Preparing For Your Lawsuit
The Inside Scoop On the Tricks of Judges, Lawyers, and Court Clerks

By: Chase Carmen Hunter

"A Handbook That Digs Into The Hidden Challenges Of Representing Yourself In Court."

The Author Is Not A Lawyer But Has Extensive Experience With The Courts And Their Clerks. This Book Will Help You Better Understand The Many Ways The Government, Including Judges And Court Clerks, Knowingly Violates The United States Constitution. It Will Show You How To Promote Your Case And Your Cause In And Out of Court. It Includes Cautions About The Risk of Retaliation By Government Officials Against Whistleblowers and Others When They Do Nothing More Than Assert Their Constitutional and Human Rights.

BONUS!!!

Get more than 1000 pages of court documents that

have been used and filed in real state and federal court cases, sample forms, and sample petitions for only $9.99 if purchased online at www.PreparingForYourLawsuit.com. You receive electronic copies and you print the documents and forms. Or you pay only $49.99 if purchased in hard-copy form. You receive printed documents and forms in the mail. If you only want documents from a specific case file, the documents can be provided at a cost of $9.99 if by delivered by email. The cost varies if you want the documents mailed.

Copyright © 2015 by Chase Carmen Hunter
First Edition 9/27/2015
All rights reserved.
ISBN-10:1517296889
ISBN-13: 978-1517296889

Table of Contents

Chapter 8

Chapter 9

Appendix A

Appendix B

Appendix C

Introduction

How To Use This Book To Prepare
For Your Civil Lawsuit

This is a handbook. It is a tool. It is designed to be small enough to literally fit comfortably in your hand so that you can easily carry it with you and learn on the run, any time, and anywhere you go. The outside margin has been slightly widened for note taking.

This is not a book about me. But I give specific examples about my experiences from which you can learn. These experiences are not unique to me. Many people have had the same experiences and didn't know how to face them and have not shared their experiences publicly.

I have read many books like this in the past that left me with more questions than answers. But this book is much different. This book will give you valuable, inside information to improve your chances if you represent yourself in court. I am not a lawyer. I am a private party who has had a great deal of experience with state and federal courts.   If a lawyer shared the information found in this book, he would likely be blackballed from the legal profession. For a lawyer, being blackballed often means that no judge will rule in the blackballed lawyer's favor; preventing the blackballed lawyer from winning any case. This book contains a wealth of information that you can't get anywhere else.

If I give you specifics about a certain case, do not make the mistake of thinking that only such circumstances can occur in that specific court. The information I am providing is specific only to illustrate the kind of experience you might have in any court.

There was a lawyer in Los Angeles, California, whose name is Richard Fine who was jailed in 2009 after he repeatedly revealed that judges in Los Angeles County were each paid about $57,000 in yearly benefits by the county. Mr. Fine asserted that under such circumstances, it was not possible to get a favorable ruling against the county. One news article located on the Internet at the link below[1] provides details that establish that Mr. Fine was essentially abducted by the court and unlawfully jailed. Fine alleged that this $57,000 in yearly benefits, which was in addition to the judges' state-paid salaries, established that the Los Angeles County judges were not able to be neutral in lawsuits seeking tax refunds or relief against the county. Sterling Norris, a lawyer for Judicial Watch, Inc., won a lawsuit on October 10, 2008, that ruled that these county payments to judges were unconstitutional: *Harold P. Sturgeon v. The County of Los Angeles* (Fourth App. Dist. Div. One, Case No. D050832)[2] Mr. Fine was jailed on March 4, 2009, after he appeared in a Los Angeles court in *Marina v. Los Angeles County*, case number BS109420. Mr. Fine's experience is just one instance that establishes the potential grave retaliation an attorney can suffer if he reveals problems

[1] "Attorney Richard Fine - dissident's false hospitalization in Los Angeles County, California*", OpEdNews,* 1/21/2010 *By Joseph Zernik* http://www.opednews.com/articles/Attorney-Richard-Fine--di-by-Joseph-Zernik-100118-435.html, last accessed 8/31/2015

[2] The court's order is included with the purchase of documents. It is 38 pages long. *See* page 1.

within the judicial system such as the ones revealed in this book.

This book shows you how the various state and federal courts abused their authority to commit crimes and protect crimes against me. While you may not be in the exact same situation, the information I am sharing is invaluable because I have had a lot of experience with the tricks of the judges and of the clerks that are used to sabotage your lawsuit.

The first rule: do not let your experiences with a rogue judge, court clerk, or public official define who you are. This means that you should not let your anger or frustration control your life.

The second rule: you are the master and the government is the servant, but always be humble.

The third rule: because a government official has authority to put you in jail (and other oppression) and you do not the have the authority to do the same to the government official, you must be mindful to approach any dispute with the government with caution even if you don't think the government official is rogue. The government official is always either rogue or prepared to be rogue when he wants to be to suit his personal agenda.

When a family member found out that I was writing this book, he said more than once that my writing this book "will get us all killed." I have been victimized by the local, state, and federal government since about 2008. The government has fabricated fraudulent court documents to empty my bank accounts, arrest me, hold me in jail, cut the locks off my house and enter for the sole purpose of kidnapping me, steal real estate that I own, and much more. All these crimes are public information because I have filed many lawsuits in state and federal courts seeking relief. Nearly every request for relief was denied. And if you studied the denials, you will see that the denials are not based in the facts or the law; therefore, the denials violated the U.S. Constitution and my human rights because at a minimum, I have a human right to expect that a court of law operates only from the truth, the facts, and the law. I believe that I have filed more than twenty federal lawsuits, not including appeals, at my last count. You can look in PACER (the Federal government's "public access to court electronic records" at www.pacer.gov) and search for a party whose name is "Hunter, Chase" (without quotes) to get a complete list of my lawsuits filed. I have a lot of experience with the tricks the judges and court clerks use to derail a lawsuit and am passing this information on to you so that you have a better understanding of the challenges you face.

I have been victimized because I have been outspoken against violations by the government of written laws and of the U.S. Constitution. And because of this, various government bodies have violated laws, committed crimes, violated the U.S. Constitution, and violated human rights treaties to retaliate against me and to silence me. When many different courts have entered orders in my lawsuits; they are most often grossly erroneous or obviously intentionally erroneous and deny me my requested relief. These court orders display a popular attitude of judges which is: "I am a judge. I have judicial immunity. I can do whatever I want. I am the law! You only get justice if I want you to get justice." It can seem like a hopeless endeavor to assert your rights when you are up against rogue government officials. Frankly, I have witnessed top-notch judges who were very fair and true to the law. But I can truthfully say that I have seen only two out of about 100 or more. Keep in mind that my experience is largely based in Virginia. As you will see in this book, many aspects of the Virginia government, not only the courts, operate without regard for the law or for the U.S. Constitution. It is the culture in Virginia. But my experience with Florida state judges and many federal judges in many other states reveal equally unlawful actions by judges and courts outside of Virginia.

Let's briefly touch on the dynamics of the U.S. Government scheme because it has much to do with the actions of a judge or court clerk   Most countries have one nation and do not have separate states.[3] Residents of these countries have only one national ID and one national driver's license. Mexico is one example of a country that has separate states and separate state ID's and driver's licenses. However, the Mexico government scheme is very different from the

[3] The CIA World Factbook can be found on the Internet and has a wealth of information on this topic.

United States. The Mexico Constitution does not give states "rights" like the U.S. Constitution does. In fact, Title V, Article 120 of the Mexico Constitution states that the governors of the States are required to publish and enforce federal laws. Other parts of Title V dictate to the states various other tasks of administrative organization. In contrast, the U.S. Constitution states in the Tenth Amendment that "[t]he powers not delegated to the United States by the Constitution, nor prohibited by it to the States, are reserved to the States, respectively, or to the people". And the U.S. Constitution gives no explicit instruction to the states regarding administration or the publishing and enforcement of federal laws. This is relevant because it demonstrates a kind of consistency and harmony among various geographic locations within Mexico, as an example of one of the few countries with separate states. In contrast, it demonstrates a kind of internal discord within the United States whereby the U.S. Constitution does not establish the federal government as the keystone of the country's government and establishes that each state is substantially, if not completely, sovereign. This is the post-civil war set-up. In order to remain as one country post-civil war, the federal government essentially promised the states that it would not intervene in state government. So, a state can legalize marijuana even though it is not legal under federal law. As another example, some states have the death penalty and some do not. Meanwhile, there is a federal death penalty for any eligible federal crime committed within any state or anywhere in the world. So, if asked, "Does the United States have the death penalty?"; the correct answer is: "Yes" if a person commits an eligible federal crime, and "Yes and No" if a person commits a state crime. It depends on the state in which the state crime was committed. This is unlike nearly every country in the world where the death penalty for any crime is established by national law.

This is quite frankly an insane government scheme. The fruit of this scheme is the creation of great confusion on what is legal and what is not. In addition, it promotes lawsuits by the states against the federal government in which the state governments can seek relief from the federal government's alleged encroachment on their rights. And what makes this scheme so illogical is that when the states file lawsuits against the federal government, they file them in federal courts whose judges were appointed by the federal government. While some might argue that the separation of powers (executive, legislative, and judicial) guarantees that a federal court is not likely to be poisoned with bias against a state government; that argument fails because federal judges are appointed by the executive branch and confirmed by the legislative branch before becoming part of the judicial branch. I laughed as I typed the previous sentence because it is a joke to believe that the three powers are truly separate. The main driver that gives any separation to the powers is the fact that each participant in the three branches of government most likely identifies as a Republican or Democrat and operates based on a loyalty to his party. The changing party majority in Congress and the changing political affiliation of the executive branch are more likely to be the only force of separation between the three branches of government. In other words, if a federal judge who is Republican was appointed by a Republican president and confirmed in a Congress whose majority membership was Republican; that judge is quite likely more inclined to rule in favor of his Republican party's position on any issue before him and rule in favor of the executive branch if the executive branch is affected by his ruling. But if time passes and the executive branch is occupied by a Democrat, the same Republican federal judge is more likely to rule against the executive branch because it is not of the same party affiliation. Political affiliation is a significant factor in the way a court rules.

Another example of a judge's bias involves local government. For example, if the county commissioner of revenue sues to collect taxes from someone; the local judge is more likely to abandon the law and rule in favor of the county commissioner because the judge wants to show his support for the government of the community which may pay his salary or provide other benefits.

Another fruit of this U.S. Government scheme that is rampant in the south includes states that blatantly ignore the U.S. Constitution in their day-to-day operation. These violations are bold and the violators have no shame. States such as Florida, Texas, Virginia, and others boldly act independently of the U.S. Constitution and of human rights treaties entered into by the United States of America. As one example, Texas violated the Vienna Convention on Consular Relations and an order issued in 2004 by the International Court of Justice[4] ("ICJ") when it executed Edgar Tamayo Arias in 2014. The Secretary of State John F. Kerry sent a letter to the then Texas Governor Perry as follows: "What the State Department is asking for is a delay in [Mr. Tamayo's] execution until he can be provided with review and reconsideration," according to Marie Harf, a State Department deputy spokesperson during a press briefing in January 2014. But the Texas governor refused to comply with the international treaty or with the order of the ICJ. The Supreme Court of the United States entered an order in 2008 in *Medellin v.*

[4] The order is included with the purchase of documents and is 61 pages long. *See* page 1.

Texas[5] in which it stated that states do not have to comply with the Vienna Convention or the order issued by the ICJ and can rely only on their state laws.

Another example involves Florida lawmakers who illegally drew congressional district boundaries to benefit the Republican party.[6] Court documents filed in December 2013 "revealed that many of the Legislature's redistricting records, including emails and other documents, were destroyed." You can read more about the subsequent litigation at this link on the Internet: http://thefloridavoter.org/redistricting-in-florida-with-the -league-of-women-voters-what-you-need-to-know/ (last accessed 8/30/3015). This is just one of the many examples of state lawmakers knowingly using their authority to commit crimes. It is important to recognize that many countries have compulsory

---

[5] The order is included with the purchase of documents and is 37 pages long. *See* page 1.
[6] *See* "Florida Illegally Drew Congressional District Boundaries To Benefit GOP, Judge Rules" at *Huffington Post*, by Ashley Alman, http://www.huffingtonpost.com/2014/07/10/florida-red istricting-gop_n_5576319.html, last accessed 8/30/2015

voting which means that all people are required to vote. Thus, this eliminates the chance for lawmakers to abuse their authority to commit crimes to inhibit voters.   Why does the United States not also have compulsory voting? Perhaps it is because those who make the laws want to   continue to unlawfully manipulate voting.

Exploring this U.S. Government scheme can help explain why some state courts of law boldly act without regard for the U.S. Constitution. Knowing this can help prepare you for just such a challenge.

Also, don't dismiss the possibility of the judge or court clerk being paid to take certain criminal actions against you.   As one example, former judge Mark A. Ciavarella, Jr. of Pennsylvania was receiving bribes for years and sending children to for-profit juvenile detention centers in violation of their constitutional rights.   On paper, there was nothing that could have been used to accuse Ciavarella of being biased against these children. Yet, he was 100% biased against them, and the victims knew that Ciavarella was biased and violating their rights but they did not know that they had available remedies to try to fight against this bias.

Many judges, if accused of bias, will most likely respond that they can only be accused of being biased based on their actions outside the court. They will most likely accuse you of trying to "judge shop" only because you don't like a ruling. But this is often just a mind game. If a judge violates the U.S. Constitution and enters a grossly erroneous court order, there is no doubt that he is biased. No citations to case law can change the U.S. Constitution which guarantees the right to an "impartial" tribunal.   And there is no possible way to classify a court as being "impartial" if it enters grossly erroneous court orders.   That fact is supported by simple logic.

Don't be afraid to use logic to support your case, and don't let the judge or court clerk play mind games with you and make you believe that your concerns have no merit.   No citation from a previous case trumps simple logic.   Every single law and every single opinion written by a court is required to be based on, among other things, logic.

However, some judges and court clerks act without regard for the U.S. Constitution and the law only because they don't like you or they don't like the issue you are supporting. Public officials violate the U.S. Constitution all the time. And many people are not well equipped to recognize these violations and not well equipped to deal with them. This book will show you the many ways that the government can and does systematically violate your constitutional rights, how you can recognize when your rights are being violated, how you can assert your rights and protect yourself, and the consequences for doing so.

Many government officials are conspiring and conspired to kidnap me and I was kidnapped for a total of eight days in 2012. I was not physically abused during my kidnappings. I was one of the lucky ones. This conspiracy to kidnap me started in about March 2012 and continues today. I will explain more about that later. But having to always worry about my safety truly challenged and challenges my emotional, physical, and intellectual balance and has absolutely destroyed many personal relationships. If you are in danger of being kidnapped or killed by a government official, you can take steps to protect yourself. But you will need a lot of stamina. Many outspoken people have been kidnapped by the U.S. Government or by state or local government. Only those who have the stamina to endure have been able to inform the public of these dangers. But most of all, if you are kidnapped (which typically, but not always, results from, for example, fraudulent arrest documents being created and disseminated to law enforcement seeking your arrest); you can not move your case forward from a jail cell (assuming that is where you are being held against your will).   If your case involves your pursuit of your constitutional or human rights, rogue government officials will possibly create circumstances that will result in your unlawful arrest, in other words, kidnapping.   This is why there is a chapter that discusses how to protect yourself from being kidnapped by rogue government officials.

As one example, Diane Booth of Hawaii, was granted political asylum in Canada in 2007 because Santa Clara County California had kidnapped her son and put him in a locked juvenile home because she refused to medicate him with Ritalin at the school's request. When she removed him from the locked juvenile home and took him to Canada, the county government accused her of parental kidnapping.

She returned to Santa Clara County California where she attempted to seek relief from the state and federal courts but the courts refused to look at her evidence and denied her relief.   But it is possible that had Diane Booth had the information in this book, she would not have accepted the courts' denials of her requests for relief, and she would have had better tools with which to move her cause forward so that she could be reunited with her son.   She has not seen her son since Santa Clara County California sent the FBI to Canada to take her son from her. A documentary film about Diane Booth and others who have suffered similar experiences can be seen online at https://youtu.be/26e5PqrCePk, written and directed by Gary Null, *The Drugging of Our Children,* last accessed 8/30/2015.

Many Americans whom I have spoken with believe that the American Revolution was borne out of the opposition to "Taxation Without Representation".   Americans often believe that the American colonists were oppressed by the King and were merely seeking revolution to secure their freedom.   Many men and women died in the

American Revolution. Therefore, asserting one's rights during the American Revolution often required one to make the ultimate sacrifice.

This book will reveal the true impetus to the American Revolution that might surprise you. History shows that the American Revolution was prompted by greed, power, disobedience, and out-right rebellion by highly-ranked government officials in and for the American colonies.

Many Americans today believe that making the ultimate sacrifice for one's freedom is reserved only for those in the military who bravely fight foreign wars. Many Americans think that fighting for one's freedom involves fighting against oppressive foreign powers. I suppose this belief comes from thinking that Americans already won their freedom at home when they won the Revolutionary War and that the only freedom fighting that remains is against foreign powers who may want to rise to oppress the United States of America.

But the reality is that Americans are secretly and severely oppressed by their local, state, and federal government every day in ways that contradict every intention of the Declaration of Independence, the U.S. Constitution, and human rights treaties.

This book will open your eyes to the ways local, state, and federal laws and rules rob Americans of their constitutional rights and human rights. It will show you the specific ways the government has knowingly and boldly abandoned the U.S. Constitution. It will show you specific ways that the courts of law commit intentional gross errors to commit and protect crimes, to violate constitutional and human rights, and to deny Americans the pursuit of justice and access to justice. It will show you specifically how those who have the power to protect Americans from violations of constitutional rights and human rights will turn a blind eye to such violations or fabricate reasons to claim that they have no power to stop such violations. Finally, this book will show you the consequences of asserting your constitutional and human rights in the United States of America. I have been kidnapped, stalked, robbed, and otherwise victimized by local, state, and federal government officials over many years only because I peacefully asserted my constitutional rights and human rights and helped educate others about their rights and how they could protect and assert their rights.

Chapter One

It is important to tell you what issue brought me front and center with a dispute with the local, state, and federal government.   It might surprise you. But before I begin, let me explain that many countries imprison outspoken people only because they are outspoken on issues the government does not want openly discussed.   As I recall, I have read news reports about China imprisoning a journalist who reported on the death of five children who were living in a dumpster.   The news reports indicate that he was imprisoned for two years because the Chinese government knew that this journalist had other similar tragedies to report. Because the Chinese government did not want this issue to be openly discussed, it silenced the journalist by denying him his liberty. Jail inmates are often denied reading glasses, writing instruments, computers, books, paper, and more. Therefore, it is physically impossible for most, if not all, inmates to continue to be outspoken from inside a jail.

I also recall reading news reports of an outspoken

person from China who was imprisoned for speaking out against the one-child law.

I have read of journalists in Russia who opposed Vladimir Putin being mysteriously shot to death in the street.

These kinds of apparent crimes and human rights violations are expected of the governments of China and Russia, right? After all, they are not the land of the free like the United States of America.

But the reality is that the United States of America readily violates its citizens' constitutional rights and human rights on the same scale as countries Americans like to denounce for having poor human rights records like China and Russia. For more information about the human rights violations of the U.S.A., visit the website of the United Nations Human Rights Office of the High Commissioner which maintains documents that provide country-specific human rights information emanating from international human rights mechanisms in the United Nations system: http://uhri.ohchr.org/ .

I am living proof of significant constitutional and human rights violations by many government officials in the United States. And the reason for this is quite simple. Some of the details are explained in court case numbers 3:12-cv-325 and 3:15-cv-206 in the U.S. District Court for the Eastern District of Virginia (in Richmond, Virginia).

I discovered that documents arising from Orange County Florida Circuit court case 2009-CA-037513 were fraudulent, and this fraud was accomplished with the help of at least two Florida state judges and at least one private-practice lawyer. Judge Thomas B. Smith's signature appears on some of the fraudulent documents. Judge Alice Blackwell knowingly signed fraudulent court orders and orders without jurisdiction that are obvious violations of the U.S. Constitution. And the Florida lawyer involved is Kenneth D. Morse. The Virginia lawyer who knowingly pursued collection of the fraudulent Florida judgment in Virginia and who made many false representations to the court is Turkessa Bynum Rollins. The Plaintiff shown on the fraudulent Florida documents is Lester Kalmanson Agency, Inc. But the president of Lester Kalmanson Agency, Inc., Mitchel Kalmanson ("Kalmanson"), was secretly added as a plaintiff by motion.

This Florida court case names me as a defendant and includes fraudulent documents that indicate that I owe the plaintiff nearly $10,000,000. The plaintiff's president, Kalmanson, then attempted to collect this fraudulent $10,000,000 judgment from my insurance policies. Obviously, Kalmanson knew the judgment documents were fraudulent and hoped that I would not uncover this fraud so that he could enrich himself fraudulently. I will explain more about this fraud later as I show you specific ways the government and the courts of law violate rights, commit intentional errors, and more to commit crimes. It is public knowledge that many fraudulent court orders have arisen from this same Florida court due to among other things, the negligence of the clerk of this Florida court.[7]

When I discovered this fraud, I began filing

---

[7] The Florida Senate Committee on Criminal and Civil Justice conducted a meeting on November 6, 2013, to discuss an examination of 7800 criminal orders arising from Orange County Florida Circuit Court that were potentially fraudulent. They ignored the fact that civil court orders were also just as potentially fraudulent.

petitions in courts of law in Virginia, where I lived, seeking relief from the fraud. And the Virginia judges violated the U.S. Constitution and my human rights to deny me relief from this obvious fraud arising from this Florida court case.

In addition, many public officials joined in the fraud against me. This fraudulent Florida judgment brought attention to the fact that I help consumers obtain liability insurance for their dogs. I am an insurance agent. I also educate consumers on their rights regarding "dangerous dog" laws. And many public officials don't want dog owners to be able to obtain such insurance or to know their rights. And Kalmanson didn't want dog owners to obtain such insurance from any other insurance provider except him; or at least, he didn't want consumers to purchase such insurance from me. There are only about three insurance providers in the country who provide such liability insurance for dog owners. And Kalmanson was losing business to me and wanted to put me out of business so that he could monopolize the insurance industry for dog owners who wanted liability insurance.

And one thing that shocks me the most is that many, if not all, public officials who knew or know about Kalmanson's insurance fraud scheme against me (by which he personally attempted to collect the fraudulent $10,000,000 judgment from my insurance policies) took no action to punish the crime and joined in the conspiracy against me to silence me, kidnap me, steal real estate from me, and much more.

Could this happen to you? Absolutely! So many government officials use their authority to commit crimes against people and against the public; and they can't be trusted. Florida lawmakers know that corruption in Florida is rampant and that Florida is classified as the most corrupt state in the United States, but they take no action to address the problems to fix them.[8]

---

[8] Florida Supreme Court record SC09-1910 ordered a statewide grand jury #19 to issue a report on its study of public corruption in Florida. The report was dated December 17, 2010, and filed with the Supreme Court of Florida on December 29, 2010. (Included for free if you purchase court documents, sample forms, and sample petitions. *See* page 1. Can be purchased separately for $9.99) In addition, on June 6, 2013, Integrity Florida published data that established Florida as the leading state

If your rights are violated and you seek relief from such violations, it is possible that the local, state, and federal public officials will seek to silence you, kidnap you, steal from you, seek to bankrupt you, stalk you, unlawfully freeze your bank accounts and assets, attack your business and more.

Frankly, if the only right that you are asserting is something that does not challenge or question the actions of a public official or a law, your risk of being retaliated against is very low. And this book will be an invaluable tool for managing your lawsuit for maximum success.

Otherwise, you must ask yourself before you decide to assert your rights against a rogue government official or an unconstitutional law, "Am I willing to lose everything as a consequence of asserting my rights?" And that is the problem for every citizen: having to decide whether or not he has the stamina, fortitude, and courage to assert a basic constitutional right and human right. By

with the most federal public corruption convictions from 2000 to 2010, according the the U.S. Department of Justice.

punishing people like me (who peacefully assert their rights) by taking everything away from them and destroying their lives, the government makes an example of them and strikes fear in all others who might get the same idea to assert their rights. As a result, citizens can be easily paralyzed by their fear and allow the "home of the free" function more like a Communist country.

But I am one of the lucky ones because I persevered and am able to write this book. I could give dozens of examples of those who lost their lives after asserting their rights. But the post-civil rights era has many examples of white and black people killed by government officials only because they exercised a basic human right. The Mississippi State Sovereignty Commission is one formal government agency that committed crimes against citizens whose only crimes were to exercise their constitutional and human rights. Many local, state, and federal government officials, in their official capacities, form a criminal enterprise. A crime is still a crime even if a public official commits the crime. But if that public official is part of the law enforcement government body or is otherwise in cooperation with the law enforcement government body, seeking relief from the crime is nearly impossible since seeking such relief requires you to ask the one who is committing the crime to also be the one who gives you relief from the crime.

Chapter Two

A quick discussion on the insurance industry will reveal that it is highly corrupt and help you to understand that insurance commissioners often work against consumers, and not on their behalf. *See* Appendix A. This is just one government authority that is statutorily obligated to protect consumers from rogue insurance companies but that serves the demands of the insurance companies at the detriment of insurance consumers. This is obvious because the National Association of Insurance Commissioners ("NAIC") is a self-regulatory, non-profit body that is designed to regulate insurance companies and agents. It is funded almost exclusively by insurance companies. History has shown that when the NAIC has wanted to impose fees or restrictions upon insurance companies, some of those same insurance companies stopped paying their fees to NAIC. Without these fees, the NAIC would cease to exist. Therefore, the NAIC reversed its position on such fees and restrictions because it could not survive the pressure inflicted upon it by the insurance companies.

Its non-profit status has never been approved by the IRS. It claims that it is a private organization and refuses to be subject to the release of information. Therefore, it operates in secret.

The NAIC regulates interstate commerce involving insurance despite the fact that United States laws prohibit any regulation of interstate commerce. The NAIC has formed model laws and pressures state lawmakers to pass the laws. For those lawmakers who refuse to pass the laws, the NAIC labels those states as non-accredited.

The NAIC also owns and operates the National Insurance Producer Registry ("NIPR") which is classified under United States law as a credit reporting agency for licensed insurance producers. It is a database that maintains information about insurance producers. And the various state insurance commissioners have knowingly reported false information about me to the NIPR. Other insurance regulators see this false information and have used it against me to penalize me and to unlawfully terminate my insurance license.

And they are violating many laws against me and

against the public because they don't want me to help dog owners obtain liability insurance. As you will see, both the insurance commissioners and the state lawmakers in many states have conspired to make it nearly impossible for dog owners to comply with "dangerous dog" laws. The intended result is to connive a reason for the local law enforcement personnel to euthanize dogs by falsely claiming that the dog owners failed to obtain liability insurance for their dogs when the truth is that some dog owners just don't qualify for such liability insurance and cannot obtain it.

All state insurance commissioners are established to protect consumers from rogue insurance companies and rogue insurance agents. Yet, the reality is that the insurance commissioners have formed the NAIC to nationalize their regulatory effort, in violation of United States laws, depend on fees from insurance companies, and have a history of giving in to the demands of insurance companies when insurance companies threaten to stop paying fees to the NAIC. Therefore, the NAIC is highly susceptible to corruption and to sacrificing the best interest of the consumer in favor of conflicting demands from insurance companies.

Chapter Three

Before I get into the details of how to prepare for your lawsuit, how to assert your rights, and how to measure the consequences beforehand; let's explore some basic steps to take to protect yourself from rogue government officials including judges, clerks of court, and any other person who is paid by taxpayers. These tips are not all-inclusive and are very general.

If you are not challenging a public official or a law, you are not likely to be in danger of retaliation for your actions. These are basic tips.

1. Always research the judge, witnesses, and opposing counsel before the deposition, hearing, trial, or any other court conference. Look for anything such as speeding tickets, home address, work address, marriage records, divorce records, career, complaints made with government agencies, judicial disclosure statements (for judges only), etc. This is important because you may need to ask a judge or lawyer to disqualify himself, for example. If a witness, judge, or lawyer has any unsavory history such as criminal

convictions, you might be able to use this to your advantage to challenge his character or ability to preside over your lawsuit.

2. Be circumspect. Speak only when necessary. Answer questions only with a "yes" or "no" if only a "yes" or "no" will suffice.

3. Never think that the more you explain your side of something, the more sympathy you will get. Every word you say will be twisted against you. Stick to the facts only. Don't share your feelings unless they describe a universal theme such as disgust for human rights violations or the demands of a civil society.

4. Be polite and non-confrontational even if under verbal attack.

5. Take notes and keep them in a safe place.

6. Record telephone conversations. It is not illegal to record telephone calls even if the other party does not consent. You record telephone calls just to personally refer back to them to refresh your memory. It can be illegal to use a recorded telephone call for any other purpose.

7. Never lie.

8. Keep written records. It is best if you scan documents and keep them in electronic storage. Always make a backup copy and keep the backup copy at someone else's residence.

9. Don't start a blog about your experience. Don't do what Barrett Lancaster Brown did in 2012 when he recorded and posted videos on YouTube stating that he was going to ruin a federal agent's life in retaliation for a search of his mother's home. Mr. Brown is now incarcerated and serving a five-year sentence. You can't move your cause forward from a jail cell because you don't have access to paper, pens, eye glasses, computers, and other tools you need.

If you are challenging a public official or a law, public officials are more likely to abuse their authority to violate your constitutional rights to silence you. Your bank accounts may be frozen or emptied, you may be kidnapped, you may be in danger of being murdered, law enforcement may enter your home by force without reason, and more.   I was personally victimized by local law enforcement which created fraudulent court documents authorizing them to cut the locks off my door to my house to search the house, without my prior knowledge. But the security system recorded the law enforcement officers' words and actions. And it proves that they entered my home unlawfully to kidnap me. This is discussed more in later chapters.

1. All of the tips above apply.

2. Live beneath your means. Just because you can afford to buy a Mercedes Benz, you shouldn't buy one. Get a car that is at least two years old and take good care of it and drive it until it dies.

3. Be self-employed if possible.   If you work in a public place, government officials know exactly where to find you, when you go to work, where you park your car, etc.

4. Get support from friends and family. This means, for example, that you should ask if you can stay with them from time to time for one day to two weeks.

5. Get to know your public transportation options including taxis and stop driving your car or drastically reduce your use of your car.

6. Make sure that your car is in perfect road

condition so that the police have no reason to stop you or anyone else driving it. And if they do, turn on your cell phone's voice or video recorder and put your cell phone on your seat.

7. Create a couple disguises including at least one that changes your gender, if possible. If you are a woman, use a mustache as part of your disguise, for example. If using a disguise, don't forget to change your posture or the way you walk and your voice. Use a different accent when you speak. The sound of a person's voice is one of the easiest ways you can be identified.

8. Never wear T-shirts or clothes that show the name of the church you go to or the name of the gym where you exercise, for example.

9. Never go to the same place two times. For example, if you need to buy stamps, don't go back to the same place you bought stamps last week. Get friends or family to get the stamps for you.

10. Never share personal information with any acquaintance. Keep to yourself.

11. Never park your car near the building you are in.

If you are going to buy an auto part, park your car at the grocery store across the street. (But first make sure that you are not being followed or watched!)

12. Always, always watch everywhere you go for people who are following you or watching you.

13. Delete your Facebook account and don't start a new one. Don't use social media.

14. Be prepared to move out of the state. It can be much easier to assert your rights involving local and state government officials when they have no access to your body.

15. Sleep fully clothed with shoes on or with shoes next to your bed if there is any danger that a rogue government official will forcibly enter your residence.

16. If you are in danger of being kidnapped by a rogue government official, always dress based on the weather outside. If it is cold and you are in the house, wear a winter hat.

17. Be patient. This process can take years. If you file a petition with a human rights organization such as the Organization of American States or the

International Court of Justice, you must first exhaust all your available remedies. And such human rights petitions can take five years or more before they are ready for review.

18. Remove all your cash from your bank accounts. Do not put this cash in anyone else's bank account. Be prepared to use only cash for a while; maybe two years or more. Don't hide your cash under your mattress or anywhere obvious.

19. Don't use credit cards. Use cash. Credit cards are tracking devices.   Give your credit card to someone you trust from time to time and let him use it so that if you credit card is being tracked, the tracker is tracking this other person and not you.

20. Don't use a cellular phone with GPS. It is a tracking device.

21. If you have a cell phone, give it to family members to carry for a couple hours, a couple days, or more so that your cell phone is not being tracked with your activities.   It is tracking someone else's activities.

22. Call your own cell phone from your home phone

sometimes and talk to your voicemail for about one minute. This can cause anyone tracking your cell phone to be confused about whether or not you are the person using your cell phone.

23. Don't do anything illegal. If you are arrested on a false charge, you will be searched. If the police find anything illegal on you during the search, the false charge is irrelevant because a valid charge has arisen from the false charge. So, if you take pain medication, make sure you don't carry a pill in your pocket because that is against the law.

24. Your house or car can be searched unlawfully at any time. Make sure you leave nothing that could be used against you. Also, stage your house and car as best you can. This means, for example, leave unopened mail addressed to someone else in your car or in your house on the table at all times. (Borrow a friend's junk mail.) Leave unopened mail addressed to you that was received months ago in other places in your house and car. Don't use your perfume or cologne and other personal items. Let dust settle on them.   Put many extra toothbrushes in every

bathroom. Don't leave your dirty clothes on the floor or in the hamper. I actually wore the same clothes everyday, washed them as needed, and put the same clothes back on for more than one year.

25. If your state has open-carry laws whereby you can legally carry an unconcealed firearm, don't do it. Any rogue police officer can claim you reached for your gun moments before he shot you dead.

26. Don't install cameras on your house unless they can't be seen from the outside.

27. Install an alarm system in your house. If the rogue police break into your home (using a fraudulent search warrant, for example), the alarm sound will at least annoy them. If your alarm system records audio or video, you can possibly record statements made that prove the police are violating your rights and/or that they know they are violating your rights.

28. Lock every single exterior door to your house with a deadbolt, a doorknob lock and at least one other lock such as a brass plate lock or a chain. Consider installing a barn door crossbar on the

inside of each exterior door.

29. Never break the law.   Don't give the police a reason to arrest you.

30. Never put yourself in close proximity to police. For example, someone I know was stopped by police for driving about 5 miles under the speed limit in the passing lane. He was stopped by state police. The state police officer stated that he would give this person a written warning and asked that he wait for the written warning in the police car.   The driver of the car went with the police officer (which was very unwise. He should have asked the police officer, "Why are you detaining me?   I will wait in my car."). While sitting in the police officer's car, the police officer's report states that he witnessed the driver's heart beating fast through the driver's shirt and saw his heart beating fast through the carotid artery in the driver's neck.   And because of this observation, the police became suspicious and asked questions such as, "Where are you going?"   The police officer asked the passenger the same question. And when the two people did

not give the same answer, the police officer became more suspicious. In the end, both the driver and passenger where arrested, spent many weeks in jail, and incurred excessive legal fees and costs. The point is that a policeman will use anything to claim that you are being suspicious and then use this fabricated suspicion to claim that he was authorized to carry out an impromptu investigation. In this situation, all the driver had to say was that he did not want to wait in the policeman's car.

31. If the police knock on your door, don't answer the door if you believe the police are rogue or intend to violate your rights. This means that you should at least go to the door and talk with the police through the closed door unless you know that the police have violated your rights or someone else's rights recently. "Violations of rights" includes police who unknowingly violate your rights or someone else's rights as can happen when police act on the orders of a rogue judge. The police in that situation are just doing their job. But their actions still violate

your rights. Do not stand at your door with the door open two inches to talk to rogue police. Do not stand in view of the rogue police inside your house and talk with them. They will likely fabricate a reason to break down your door such as falsely claiming that you pointed a gun at them from inside the house. Don't open the door even if they tell you that they have a warrant. Police can and do lie all the time. Let them break down your door or let them go away.

32. Always carry an emergency pack on your body or in your pocket (but not in a purse which is not attached to your body) which includes a small flash light, a throw-away cell phone purchased and activated by someone else (and not in your name or any family member's name) that has never been used, keys to various friends and family member's homes and to a car, and a prepaid VISA with a $15-$80 balance.

33. Whenever you go anywhere, give someone you are with your wallet or purse so that if you are arrested, these items won't be taken from you and held by the jail. If these items are held by the

jail, your spouse may not have access to the cash, credit cards, and car keys.

34. Always wear three shirts of different designs and colors so that if you are being pursued, you can take the top shirt off to change your appearance. If you are a woman, also wear a skirt that is floor-length and wear shorts, pants, or leggings underneath it so that you can take the skirt off to change your appearance.

35. Always wear running shoes...for running fast as you can.

36. Use the Freedom of Information Act or Open Records Act whenever you want or need information on any public agency that may help your cause or affect you.

37. Overpay your taxes slightly. If you are an employee, slightly reduce your number of exemptions so that you overpay your taxes slightly. You will be eligible for a refund. If you are delayed in filing your annual tax return, you can be accused of doing so to avoid timely payment of taxes. But if you overpaid your taxes, this accusation will fail. You may be delayed in

filing your annual returns for many reasons. But you also may want to purposely delay your filing of your annual returns for many reasons. Intentionally delaying the filing of your annual tax returns is likely a misdemeanor. But if you don't file taxes on time, the only person who suffers is you since you are overpaying your taxes and are due a refund. So, you are unlikely to be charged with a misdemeanor. One reason why you may want to delay your tax filing is to give yourself a couple months to move to a different jurisdiction to avoid rogue government officials from using your tax returns to create reasons to harass you. I once disputed a business license tax charged by my local commissioner of revenue in Fredericksburg, Virginia in 2007. She knowingly charged me about $4000 for a tax that I was not required to pay. I subsequently sued because the treasurer would not refund to me the overpaid tax. I subsequently received most of the refund that I was seeking; not because I won the lawsuit. The judge (William Jerome Cox, who was retired, and now deceased) ruled against me for reasons not based in the law. The treasurer refunded most of what I requested prior to the trial date. But after that time of my outspokenness against paying a tax that I was not required to pay, the commissioner of revenue began charging me personal property tax for cars I did not own. I refused to pay this tax. The treasurer then blocked my ability to renew my auto registration. I then paid the tax I was not required to pay just so that I could renew my auto registration. But the treasurer denied receiving my payment even though I paid electronically and had proof that the debit was made from my bank account. But the treasurer still refused to unblock my auto registration. I went to the Commissioner of the Department of Motor Vehicles who called the treasurer on the telephone in my presence and told the treasurer that I was not past due on my personal property taxes and that he had five minutes to unblock my auto registration. The treasurer unblocked my auto registration. The treasurer was a rogue government official who repeatedly kept and collected taxes from me to which he was not entitled and to which he knew he was not entitled.

38. If you get your car oil changed, for example, don't give the repair shop your real name. They don't need it. Use an alias. If you drop off film to be developed or clothes to be dry cleaned, for example, don't use your real name. If you use any services where you have to wait for your name to be called, use an alias. This is not possible in a doctor/hospital setting. But if you are at the veterinary clinic or a restaurant, for example, don't use your real name. If you bank at one of those banks where the employees think that greeting you loudly by name in a crowded bank branch lobby is part of good customer service, don't go to that bank branch or politely and softly tell the employee that you don't want to be called by your name for privacy reasons.

39. Search online for stories about other people whose constitutional and human rights were violated and who survived. Find out how other people survived or thrived. One time I watched a long and boring video of a woman who

described how her constitutional and human rights were violated because she was going through a divorce with a man who was Christian and she wanted to raise their baby Jewish. This man had ties to the law enforcement and legal community. She ended up in jail for about one year with about 28 felony charges; during which time another baby she gave birth to died while in someone else's care. All felony charges were dropped. Her name is Valerie Carlton. Although the video I watched on the Internet was long and boring, I clung to every word for hints on how I could survive my ordeal. And the video was helpful. So, be patient and you will find more helpful tips on the Internet. *See* more about Valerie's story in Appendix B.

I read a news story about a man named Herb Lux of Spotsylvania, Virginia, who was in dispute with the local prosecutor because the man's son was arrested and imprisoned based on what the man believed was insufficient evidence. *See* Appendix C. This dispute carried on for years and resulted in the man being charged and convicted of crimes and being sentenced to jail.

This man did everything wrong. He used social media and blogs to complain about the prosecutor. He boldly violated court orders requiring him to stay away from jurors who decided his son's fate. He told jurors things that were not revealed in the trial and tried to ask them if they still would have found his son guilty if they had known this information. He somehow thought that he could effect change upon the rogue prosecutor with his actions. The prosecutor took steps against Herb Lux that violated his constitutional rights and human rights and seemed to have admitted that he was retaliating against Mr. Lux due to his blogs. But none of that matters if the man is in jail. There is nearly nothing Mr. Lux can do to assert his rights from jail.

Another real-life tragedy involving Behzad Samimi of Springfield, Massachusetts, illustrates my point well. Mr. Samimi was severely beaten by employees of a government official in 2010. He was accused of trespassing at a democratic party event. He was a supporter of the democratic party and was there to show his support. It seems as if Mr. Samimi was targeted because he is outspoken about many things as you will discover if you read a complaint Mr. Samimi filed in a U.S. District Court. (The complaint is available for purchase. *See* page 1.) Mr. Samimi's complaint has been pending for many years. After reading Mr. Samimi's complaint, I conclude that Mr. Samimi was victimized horribly by employees of government officials but that he has never been his own best advocate. He seems to continually put himself in a confrontational situation with government officials with the unfortunate belief that the U.S. Constitution alone permits him to be confrontational without consequences. While in theory, this is true; in practice, it is very dangerous as Mr. Samimi has learned first hand. Mr. Samimi's beating has rendered him permanently disabled and in need of daily care.

Even if you are right about an issue, you must assert yourself peacefully and be smart about it. Follow these tips in this chapter. No matter what you do, your story will not make the first page of the newspaper, you won't garner public support, your rights will continue to be violated, and the rogue public officials will not lose their jobs. I read a news article in June 2015 about Florida prisons and the federal government's investigation into why a high number of Florida inmates are dying. The evidence shows that many prisoners have died because of violence committed against them by prison employees. As a result of this investigation and revelation, many of these prison employees were fired; not criminally prosecuted.

Also, Sun-Ming "Sunny" Shue, from New York, is a fine example of the grave consequences for a man who asserted his rights. He mysteriously died on June 26, 2010, in a street due to blunt force trauma within three days of publishing a video on the Internet in which he said, "Now I have enough evidence to put [New York Judge] Golia in jail". Mr. Shue was wrong to think that he had sufficient evidence to cause the Department of Justice to criminally investigate and to criminally charge Judge Golia whom he believed was a corrupt judge. It is a mistake to think that someone outside the brotherhood of lawyers had such power by simply showing that Judge Golia committed a felony when he did not truthfully disclose his financial condition on his New York judge's financial disclosure statement. Also, a personal attack on any public official such as stating, "Now I have enough evidence to put [New York Judge] Golia in jail," did not move Mr. Shue's cause forward and will not move your cause forward. In addition, Judge Golia's omissions from his financial disclosure statement had no link to Mr. Shue's cause. If Mr. Shue could show, for example, that Judge Golia failed to disclose substantial stock ownership in XYZ Company and this same XYZ Company was a party to a lawsuit Mr. Shue filed that was assigned to Judge Golia, then perhaps Mr. Shue could have sought relief from Judge Golia's unfair rulings on this basis. That was the only best option at that time for Mr. Shue. He also could have filed petitions of appeal, petitions with the New York judge ethics commission, and a petition with a human rights organization (which takes several years to be reviewed). But unless you can show that a judge accepts bribes, for example, you should not attempt to find a way to have a judge criminally charged. Remember, the people who would criminally charge him are possibly longtime friends.

Judge Golia retired in 2012 and now works as a lawyer for Finz & Finz in New York. And Mr. Shue is dead.

There was an alarming degree of concern from the federal courts in August 2014 when a U.S. District Court judge in Alabama, Mark Fuller, was accused, not convicted, of battery. The Eleventh Circuit Court of Appeals reassigned all Judge Fuller's cases and at least one U.S. Senator, Richard Shelby of Alabama, called for Judge Fuller to resign. Judge Fuller was not subsequently convicted. And many U.S. Congressmen made public statements upon learning of his arrest that claimed that Judge Fuller's actions (which were only allegations) betrayed the public's trust in him as a judge. Yet, many federal judges enter grossly erroneous court orders and use their authority to commit and support crimes and to violate the U.S. Constitution and human rights; and U.S. Congressmen make no statements and take no action. As you will read in Chapter Five, the Eleventh Circuit Court of Appeals is classified by the author as one of the worst courts in the country (under subheading: Florida state and federal courts).

The government will not hesitate to ruin your life just for fun.   Let's look at Mr. Lux's situation above and in Appendix C. Even if Mr. Lux wins in the end, he will spend a lot of money on legal fees, bail bonds, and many other costs.   He is retired; so, the criminal charges won't cause him to lose his job. But he could possibly be bankrupted. He could lose his house and everything he owns to bankruptcy.   (Virginia's homestead exemption is only $5000.) And worse still, his joy in life will have been destroyed by his fight with the government. What is the reward in the end if Mr. Lux is victorious? Personal satisfaction?   I am not convinced that personal satisfaction is a good enough reason.   But if you have a passion for an issue and you are willing to sacrifice everything for it, then fighting the government may be worth it to you. Perhaps Mr. Lux's purpose was to expose the theatrical nature of his son's criminal trial.   Many criminal trials are not based on the truth as much as they are based on which witness the jury likes the most, or who lies the best, or whether or not the jury likes the criminal defense lawyer, for example. Sometimes exculpatory evidence is hidden by the prosecutor, or certain significant evidence is withheld from the jury; and the trial is very unfair. But Mr. Lux's attempt to personally visit with the jurors in his son's trial to explain his thoughts on these issues was an unfortunate choice for addressing the issues. And it changed nothing about how his son's trial was handled. The only fruit of his actions was criminal charges, criminal convictions, legal fees, the cost of bail bonds, and more.

The point is this: if you are already in a dispute with the government through no fault of your own and you are an innocent victim, you might not have much to lose in continuing to fight for your rights. The government may have already caused you to lose everything you have. But if you are not yet in a dispute with the government and are considering your options to fight for your rights; don't be foolish and think that you have the U.S. Constitution on your side. Consider the consequences first because the writings of Franz Kafka's *Der Process* (The Trial) are oftentimes the reality when dealing with the U.S. government and its courts of law. This book will help you to come to the right decision for you and your family and give you tools for making your way through your fight.

Chapter Four

You will need to accept that your constitutional and human rights are not always freely given by the U.S. Government and other governments operating inside the U.S.A. You must fight for your rights at your own expense. And the cost is high. Remember, fighting for your rights can require the ultimate sacrifice: death.

It is not my intention to discourage you from fighting for your rights. This book will teach you how to skillfully, peacefully, and patiently fight for your rights while keeping yourself as safe as possible. Many whistleblowers and activists have successfully survived. The Rutherford Institute in Charlottesville, Virginia, is one example of an organization that is outspoken against the government's violations of constitutional rights. John Whitehead is the leader of The Rutherford Institute and he has two publications which reveal his grave concerns about the U.S. government: *Government of Wolves* and *Battlefield America.* I have not discovered any ways in which Mr. Whitehead has suffered for being outspoken. However, Mr. Whitehead is a lawyer, and quite possibly, he is immune from such attacks since such attacks are almost always launched and supported by lawyers. (Don't forget that judges are lawyers.) One common theme you will discover in this book is that lawyers stick together and are a brotherhood. Any strong organization, including the likes of the mafia and street gangs, is built on a foundation of brotherhood and protecting the brotherhood at all cost.

The list of tricks that some courts and law enforcement will use to deny you your rights is very long. And I will share all that I know and have experienced. But I will start with the most obvious ways and you can order the court records if you want more details. *See* page 1.

1. The judge will knowingly sign a fraudulent court order. This happened to me many times. Here is one good example. In Chesterfield County Virginia Circuit Court case CL14-1255, the judge, Steven C. McCallum, signed a court order on January 7, 2015, that he knew had been forged by Turkessa Bynum Rollins. The court order shows that Ms. Rollins signed as counsel for the

plaintiff, Lester Kalmanson Agency, Inc., and that she forged the signature of the counsel for the defendant. And she did this in front of the judge, before the judge signed the court order. (Typically, in Virginia, the judge directs the parties sign the order, and then he signs the order. Even if the judge did not see Ms. Rollins forge Ms. Gring's signature, he knew when he signed the court order that Ms. Gring was not present at the hearing and that her signature could not have appeared on the court order unless it was forged.) I know that Ms. Rollins forged the signature of the counsel for the defendant because a) the handwriting for Ms. Rollins' signature and for opposing counsel, Kelly Gring is similar, and b) to the right of Kelly Gring's forged signature is printed the following: "by TBR w/permission". TBR stands for Turkessa Bynum Rollins. This means that Ms. Rollins signed Ms. Gring's signature on the court order and claims that she had the authority to do so because Ms. Gring gave Ms. Rollins, opposing counsel, permission to do so. This is a crime.

It is forgery. And it proves that two officers of the court, Steven C. McCallum and Turkessa Bynum Rollins conspired and forged and permitted the forging of another lawyer's signature on a court order. This fraudulent court order was later presented as a valid court order by various people in Virginia to steal real estate from me.

2. The court will enter a final, appealable order and not inform you about this event. This happened to me in the United States District Court for the District of Columbia did this in my lawsuit 1:14-cv-00707.

3. The court will refuse to enter a final appealable order. This happened to me in Chesterfield County (Virginia) Circuit Court case CL13-225 in an order dated 3/15/13 and entered by Judge Steven Colin McCallum. You cannot appeal unless there is a final appealable order except under federal rules which allow you to appeal after 150 days of a court's final, appealable decision if an appealable order is not entered. *See* Federal Rules of Civil Procedure 58(c) and

58(d) at http://www.law.cornell.edu.

4. The court will sanction you for reasons for which there is no evidence and for reasons for which you cannot be sanctioned. For example, a court sanctioned me only because I appealed to the Supreme Court of the United States. This happened to me in Chesterfield County (Virginia) Circuit Court case CL13-225 in an order dated 3/15/13 and entered by Judge Steven Colin McCallum. One of the reasons for granting unlawful sanctions is to fraudulently enrich counsel for the party who seeks sanctions and to intimidate a party who has a valid complaint.

5. The clerk of the court will lose your court file while the adverse party is filing documents into this same file. Therefore, when you go to the clerk's office to review the file, you are denied the review and are being blocked from knowing that the adverse party is filing documents in your case. This happened to me in City of Fredericksburg (Virginia) Circuit Court case CL11-358, where the clerk of that court is Jeff Small, a Virginia attorney, and former assistant

Commonwealth Attorney.

6. The court ignores a properly filed and noticed motion. Many courts have ignored motions I properly filed and noticed. In Henrico County (Virginia) Circuit Court case CL12-1831, the judge, Gary A. Hicks, ignored every single motion I filed and properly noticed. And the Supreme Court of Virginia denied my appeal on June 14, 2013, in appeal number 13-0161.

7. The judge denies a properly filed and noticed motion by voicemail. In Henrico County (Virginia) Circuit Court case CL12-1831, I received a voicemail message from a court employee telling me that the judge denied my motion for a temporary restraining order. You cannot appeal a voicemail message.

8. The judge will deny you access to the court file. In Henrico County (Virginia) Circuit Court case CL12-1831, the judge, Gary A. Hicks, kept the court file in chambers at all times. Each time I went to the clerk's office to see the file, I was denied access to it on the basis that the file was in the judge's chambers.

9. The court ignores emergency motions. Many courts have ignored my emergency motions. This allowed the crimes being committed against me by public officials to continue. Therefore, the courts that ignored and ignore my emergency motions are explicitly supporting the crimes being committed. As one example, the Virginia Supreme Court ("VSC") never ruled on my emergency motion to stay filed in August 2012 in petition 12-1405 which asked the court to direct a circuit court judge in City of Fredericksburg (Virginia) Circuit Court case CL11-358 to cease attempts to arrest me using fraudulent court documents. The VSC entered only one order denying the petition. It was entered on December 21, 2012, after the judge had already arrested me and after the judge had terminated his commission to preside over the case.

10. The judge enters an order but does not deliver it to the court clerk until after the time for filing an appeal expires. This happened to me in City of Fredericksburg (Virginia) Circuit Court case CL11-358 and the judge was Jonathan C.

Thacher (retired). The judge dated the signed order on about January 3, 2013, but did not deliver it to the clerk of the court, Jeff Small, until after April 3, 2013, which was past the 90-day time-frame during which an appeal could be filed.

11. The court enters a court order that makes blatantly false conclusions and factual statements. You must understand that when other courts review your case file (upon appeal, for example), they often rely only upon the court orders. So, a court order with false statements can be the death of your lawsuit. This happened to me many times. As one example, in United States District Court for the Middle District of Florida case 5:14-cv-00410, the judges repeatedly entered court orders that explicitly stated that they believed only some of my claims were not viable but also explicitly stated that my lawsuit was frivolous. Obviously, if the judges found only some of my claims nonviable, the remaining claims were viable. Therefore, it is not possible that my lawsuit was frivolous. As another

example, Judge Richard Mills of the U.S. District Court for the Central District of Illinois entered a grossly false court order in case 14-3324 on April 4, 2015, when he stated in the order that the case came to a trial or hearing and that the lawsuit had been fully adjudicated when the truth is that adverse party had never been served with the summons and complaint and no hearings or trial were held.

12. The court enters a court order and supports its decision with citations to case law that have no relation to the facts and law of the lawsuit. Always check the citations to monitor the use of this trick by the courts. Always immediately file a motion to vacate such orders and explain that the citations don't apply to your lawsuit. Be specific. Here is one of many examples in my experience: The record in appeal number 14-15543 in the Eleventh Circuit Court of Appeals includes an order filed on July 21, 2015, that is grossly erroneous. It is signed by Circuit Judge Julie Carnes. On the top of page 4 of 9 of this July 21, 2015, order, it states that the court relied upon *Martinez* 364 F.3d to deny

my request to proceed *in forma pauperis* and it misquoted *Martinez* 364 F.3d to support its denial. This July 21, 2015, order misquotes *Martinez* as follows: "explaining that, in civil case seeking damages, 'courts should grant the privilege (pauper status) sparingly'." The accurate quote from *Martinez* provides a completely different meaning which is: "[a] trial court has wide discretion in denying an application to proceed IFP under 28 U.S.C. § 1915. This is especially true, the rubric goes, in civil cases for damages, wherein the courts should grant the privilege sparingly. However, in denying such applications a court must not act arbitrarily. Nor may it deny the application on erroneous grounds." The full quote from *Martinez* has a much different meaning than Circuit Judge Julie Carnes' misquote. In addition, the lawsuit in question was not only seeking damages. It also sought a declaratory judgment and injunctive relief involving my constitutional rights and human rights.

13. The clerk of the court enters a letter stating that the court made a decision in your case but there is no order that reflects the clerk's statement.

Always file a motion asking that the clerk provide you with the court order.

14. The court enters a fraudulent court order declaring that a *pro se* party is in contempt of court. While the *pro se* party knows that he was not in contempt of court, or that he was not advised of the allegation against him and not given a chance to defend the allegation (with a hearing or trial and with legal representation); that is not going to help in the immediate term. If you are representing yourself and found in contempt of court and sentenced to 30 days in jail, you will be unable to assert or protect your rights and your lawsuit will be dismissed, or a judgment will be entered against you while you are in jail. Typically, the court will want to sentence a *pro se* party who has a valid claim or defense to a long time in jail so that the statute of limitations will expire while he is in jail or he will lose his job and be bankrupt while in jail and his life will be so completely ruined that pursuing his cause will no longer be of interest after he is released from jail.

a) On this point: Control Your Temper! Never, never believe that being acrimonious or aggressive with a judge is clever. It is quite lethal. A judge could find you in contempt of court and sentence you to 12 months in jail if you, for example, use profanity in his court or use an aggressive, disrespectful tone.

15. The court enters fraudulent court orders against parties who have never been served with process and have no idea that action is being taken against them. This happened to me many times. Orange County Florida Circuit Court case 2009-CA-037513 is one example.

16. The court enters a fraudulent court order declaring that a *pro se* party is in contempt of court so that a *pro se* party who may be hard to find to serve with civil process can be pursued by law enforcement, arrested, and served with civil process while handcuffed. This happened to me when a Florida court (Orange County Florida Circuit Court 2009-CA-037513) conspired with a Virginia court (City of Fredericksburg case CL11-358). The Florida court had no

jurisdiction over me and had entered court orders against me. In an attempt to try to fix this problem, the Virginia court entered fraudulent court orders seeking my arrest. When I was in handcuffs, the local police called a private process server who came to the location of my arrest and served me with papers in the Florida civil lawsuit which was almost two years after the final judgment had already appeared in the record in the Florida lawsuit. The police literally held me in handcuffs for about ten minutes, outside the police car, so that they could force me to wait for the private process server to come give me papers in the fraudulent Florida lawsuit. Obviously, the Florida court knew it had been involved in substantial criminal activity and was trying to force my appearance in this civil court which had no jurisdiction over me. There was no proof in the Florida lawsuit that I had been served with the lawsuit before the final judgment was allegedly entered. In addition, the Florida court and the Virginia court falsely accused me of doing things that they used to fraudulently justify using law enforcement to arrest me. As one example, both civil courts scheduled hearings on the same morning of the same day in which they expected me to appear (even though I had not been summonsed to appear). It is not humanly possible to appear in two different courts at the same time. Subsequently, both courts either found me in contempt of court in my absence or sought the same. In addition, another fruit of such fraud is to cause the fraudulent arrest of a party, handcuff them, and create reasons to charge them with crimes. If a search of a handcuffed person turns up a pain pill in a back pocket; a criminal charge can be lodged for this crime even though the initial arrest was fraudulent. Some municipalities do body cavity searches and other humiliating things. Yet another benefit to this fraud is to force a party over whom a court has no jurisdiction to appear against his will before that court solely so that the court can claim that it has jurisdiction over that person. If the court issues an arrest warrant, the warrant will typically tell the police to bring the arrested person to see a specific judge in a specific court. Once the arrested person is delivered against his will, the court will use that opportunity to steal jurisdiction over that person.

17. The court enters court orders that are grossly erroneous. What you need to know is that these erroneous court orders may be relied upon by others as being valid. The fact is that they are not valid and they are void. But if you try to explain this to other unlawful courts of law, they will turn a blind eye to the fact that the court order is obviously erroneous and treat it as if it is valid. In addition, if the aggrieved party appeals the erroneous court order, the appeal alone could take one year. In the meantime, the relief the lawsuit requests can be delayed during the appeal. Even if the party asks for injunctive relief during the appeal, such a request will most likely be denied so that the aggrieved party is denied any and all kind of prompt relief. If the courts can delay granting relief for many years, it is the equivalent of denying relief.

18. Clerks of courts will refuse to perform ministerial duties and block your lawsuit in every possible way. The clerks of the courts are most often friends with the judges and are not independent actors. One example of this can be seen in U.S. District Court cases 1:14-cv-510 and 1:15-cv-405 in the Western District of Texas. These lawsuits prove that the clerk of the Travis County (Texas) District Court (state court), Amalia Rodriguez-Mendoza (retired) and Velva L. Price, refused to perform ministerial duties in lawsuits I filed against the Texas Department of Insurance. A review of these lawsuits shows that the district judges, Andrew W. Austin and Lee Yeakel, entered grossly erroneous court orders to deny me relief from the state clerks' refusal to comply with my Due Process rights. This is one example in which the federal courts support the criminal activities of the state's local public officials.

19. Judges will ignore every properly filed motion filed by a party who is fighting for his rights and grant every motion filed by the adverse party.

This is obvious in many lawsuits in which I filed especially Henrico County (Virginia) Circuit Court case CL12-1831 in which Gary A. Hicks was the judge.

20. Judges will deny your request for a hearing and grant the adverse party's request for a hearing, thereby, denying you a chance to have your motion heard. This happened to me in Chesterfield County (Virginia) Circuit Court case CL11-2361 over which retired judge Michael C. Allen was presiding. The judge will claim that his schedule does not allow enough time for both motions to be heard. If the other party's motion is a motion to dismiss, the judge will dismiss your lawsuit. Meanwhile, your motion that the judge refused to hear is a motion for an order of default. If the judge had heard only your motion (which you filed before the other party filed a motion to dismiss); the judge would have been squeezed into a corner to grant your motion for default. But by denying your motion to be heard, the judge denies your motion by dismissing the lawsuit before your motion can be

heard. I petitioned the Virginia Supreme Court ("VSC") in petition 12-0577 to direct this circuit court judge to stop blocking my motions from being heard. The Virginia attorney general supported the judge's actions as a "scheduling" issue. And the VSC denied my petition on the false basis that mandamus is not a substitute for appeal. The fact is that if the judge was blocking my access to the court, that requires immediately relief and is not the kind of circumstance that can be delayed to be addressed only upon appeal.

21. Judges will enter non-public (secret) orders directing the clerks of court not to file documents received by a *pro se* party. The United States District Court for the District of Columbia did this in my lawsuit 1:14-cv-00707. And when I appealed to the circuit court of appeals, it stated only that I was not prejudiced by the district court's unlawful actions. It made no attempt to direct the district court to correct its errors. I was told by an anonymous woman who works in the "*pro se*" unit of this district court that nothing received from a "*pro se*" party

is filed automatically except a notice of appeal. Therefore, when I filed, for example, notices of my change of address, they were not filed. And the record establishes that an anonymous judge told the clerk verbally not to file my notice of address change (and other documents). This is established in the record because I have date-stamped copies of documents from this district court proving that this district court received my documents but these documents don't appear in the file. And when I raised this issue upon appeal and included copies of my date-stamped documents, this district court then began refusing to date-stamp and return to me upon my request any copies of documents I mailed to it.

22. The court will twist your petition into something that it is not. In the District of Columbia Circuit Court of Appeals appeal number 14-5149, the court twisted my petition for a declaratory judgment into a petition for a writ of mandamus. This unlawful action denied me my constitutional right to petition the government

for redress of my grievances (under the First Amendment). There is a huge difference between a petition for a declaratory judgment and a petition for a writ of mandamus.

23. Clerks of courts will summons your family members to serve jury duty even though those family members don't live in the clerks' jurisdictions. They do this to fabricate a reason to issue a summons for your family member's arrest for his/her failure to appear. Or another reason for this is to force your family member to appear in the court only to serve papers for you upon your family member.

24. Clerks of court will file a motion as a notice of appeal or file it as a page of a notice of appeal and never notify the court that a motion is pending. This happened to me in U.S. district court for the Eastern District of Virginia in Richmond case 3:14-cv-648.

25. Judges will conspire with attorneys to enter fraudulent court documents. This happens all the time. Make sure that you review your court record once each week. This happened to me in

Chesterfield County (Virginia) Circuit Court case CL11-2361. The judge, Michael C. Allen (retired), conspired with John Randolph Smith of Smith & Wells, PC, in Midlothian, Virginia, to enter a final order the day after the real final order was entered. This fraudulent final order dispensed with my signature and gave the false impression that I had not preserved my objections for appeal.

26. Courts will enter final orders and never notify the plaintiff of the final order so that the plaintiff does not know that an appealable event has occurred. This happened to me in the U.S. District Court for the District of Columbia, case 1:14-cv-707.

27. Courts will enter orders that make it seem like a lawsuit is dismissed and that an appealable event has occurred when the lawsuit has not been dismissed. For example, the court will enter an order stating that the lawsuit will be dismissed at some date in the future if the plaintiff does not act by that date. Before that date arrives, the clerk of the court will enter a note in the docket

stating that the case was dismissed when it was not. This happened to me in U.S. district court for the Eastern District of Virginia in Richmond case 3:14-cv-648. Then the court will enter an order denying a motion on the basis that the lawsuit had been dismissed when there is no order in the record that states that the case is dismissed. If a plaintiff attempts to appeal this fake dismissal, the appeal will be denied. The appellate court may not explain why the appeal was denied. But presumably, the basis for such a denial is that the lower court's actions are not appealable because no final, appealable order had been entered.

28. A U.S. Magistrate judge will enter an order that he has no authority to enter. This happened to me many times. The U.S. Code is very clear regarding a U.S. Magistrate judge's authority. In general, 28 U.S.C § 636 et seq. only permits U.S. Magistrate judges to rule on non-dispositive matters. *See* http://www.law.cornell.edu to read federal laws and rules.

29. The clerk will show in the record that a

document you sent to the court has only been received which means that it is not "filed" and will not be given to the court for consideration. If you see this, contact the court clerk and resolve this issue so that your document is "filed". There is a huge difference between "received" and "filed".

30. The clerk administrator will schedule your motion to be heard by a judge in a different court from the one in which your case is pending. That judge and that court does not have jurisdiction. That judge will deny the requested relief which could lead the movant to believe that he can appeal this denial. The movant may then be tricked into appealing from the court in which his case is pending. The appellate court will then deny relief without explanation. But the reason for the appellate denial is that the appellate court has no jurisdiction to hear an appeal from the wrong court in which the clerk administrator scheduled the movant's hearing. This happened to me in Travis County (Texas) District Court ("TCTDC") case

D-1-GN-13-002576 and D-1-GN-13-001957. The court administrator fraudulently scheduled my hearings with a "county court" judge. I spoke with Laurie in TCTDC administration in August 2015 and told her that I wanted to (re)schedule my motions. She claimed that my motions had already been heard. I explained that they had not been heard because the court administrator caused my motion to be transferred to a county court which had no jurisdiction to hear the motions. Laurie claimed that TCTDC local rule 1.3 allowed for such a transfer to a county court. But it doesn't. Local rule 1.3 (effective 2014) states only that any judge "among the District Courts" can hear motions. If I had tried to appeal the fraudulently-obtained "county court" order to the Texas Third Court of Appeals, that appeals court would deny my appeal on the basis that it does not have appellate jurisdiction over a "county court".

31. The judge will ask the *pro se* party questions that seem helpful but are not helpful and that amount

to bad legal advice. One example is, "Do you want to attach a copy of your objections to the order?" Another example, "You can write your objections on the order." This happened to me in City of Fredericksburg (Virginia) Circuit Court case CL11-358, with Judge Gordon F. Willis[9].

---

[9] Gordon F. Willis' father, Jere M.H. "Mac" Willis Jr. was a judge for the Virginia court of appeals. He retired in 2002. He is the son and grandson of lawyers. *See* Virginia State Bar article at: http://www.vsb.org/site/news/item/carrico-award-2010 / (last accessed 9/2/2015). The elder Willis had been a member of the Fredericksburg Virginia City Council and had been a Virginia Commonwealth Attorney prior to becoming a judge. He retired in 2002. Gordon F. Willis' wife, Victoria A. B. Willis, was elected in 2014 for a Virginia judgeship and was an attorney in the City of Fredericksburg for Durette Crump PLC prior to accepting the judgeship. While *Virginia Lawyers Weekly* once published details regarding the election process for state judges, the Virginia General Assembly, which elects judges, now conducts the election process in secret. In fact, the Virginia Division of Legislative Services no longer publishes the election results on its website at http://www.dls.virginia.gov. I have visited this website often (last accessed 9/2/15) and find that it hasn't been updated in about two years or more. In recent years, I had asked the Virginia General Assembly to allow me to testify against the re-election of some of the judges named in this book. All but one retired before I could testify. Judge

This is a trick because the judge will have your attached objections filed separately from his order which will give the impression that the *pro se* party made no objections to the judge's order. Contemporaneous objections are required for appellate review. If the *pro se* party does not preserve his objections in the record, the appellate court cannot review those errors. If you only write your objections on the order, any

Gordon F. Willis is the only judge against whom I testified against by affidavit. And he was re-elected. I believe that this secrecy has possibly arisen from the many complaints that I have filed against Virginia judges. In a news article published by *The Daily Press* in September 2014, the author, Travis Fain, reported the following:: "This was my first time following judicial elections in Virginia. It's hard to follow, seemingly by design. Legislators discuss decisions in secret, some candidates get a brief public interview before a joint committee, then it's a block vote by the full House and Senate to elect judges en masse, for the most part. Legislators I spoke to this week typically weren't willing to discuss, on the record, details of individual elections, or to explain how they reached a decision." *See* "Full List of Virginia Judges", *The Daily Press*, at http://www.dailypress.com/news/politics/shad-plank-blo g/dp-full-list-of-new-virginia-judges-20140919-post.html, last accessed 9/2/2015.

objections you made in previous court documents that you forget to include on the order are not preserved for appellate review. Also, any oral objections you made that you forget to include on the order are not preserved for appellate review. The better way to preserve objections is to sign your name on the bottom of the court order before the judge signs it and write these words immediately next to your name, "seen and objected to for the reasons stated on the record." You can also add any additional objections on the court order. While it is not wrong to attach a separate document containing objections to a court order, you must make a specific reference on the order, next to where you signed your name, such as, "seen and objected to for the reasons stated on the record and on the attached ____-page [enter the number of pages of the list of objections] list of ____ [enter a number of objections on the list] objections".

32. As you will note in footnote 9, the Virginia state lawmakers have unlawfully made secret the

election process for judges. There are many features of the Virginia state government whereby significant government agencies, such as the Virginia State Corporation Commission ("SCC") which is the umbrella for multiple unrelated state agency operations, operate in secret and refuse to be subject to the state's Freedom of Information Act ("VFOIA"). And this secrecy was supported by the Virginia Supreme Court in *George H. Christian v. State Corporation Commission*, in record 10-2477, and by the lawmakers (i.e. The General Assembly, i.e. Legislators) who have failed to pass legislation correcting the Virginia Supreme Court's ruling. The federal FOIA gives the public the right to request access to records from any federal agency. The FOIA keeps citizens informed about federal government activity. But the U.S. Constitution allows states to make their own laws even if they contradict federal laws. The U.S. Constitution establishes that the government is the servant and the people are the master. And it is sinister when the Virginia government or any government operates in secret because, among other things, it denies the citizens the right to know what the few members of the government are doing that affects the life, liberty, and freedom of all citizens. The VFOIA (Virginia Code Section 2.2-3700 et. seq.) explicitly states that it applies to every "Public body" which "means any legislative body, authority, board, bureau, commission, district or agency...." Yes, despite this unambiguous statute, the SCC claims that it is not subject to the VFOIA and the Virginia Supreme Court refused to enter a ruling that was based on this plain language. I share this with you because if your lawsuit challenges the government or a law, you can make requests for information under the state or federal freedom of information act that can be used as evidence in your lawsuit. The government in Virginia (and many other states) does whatever it wants, regardless of the law or the U.S. Constitution; and your request under the freedom of information act may be ignored. When the Virginia government has been challenged on certain issues, it simply locked its doors to the public by, for example, re-electing state judges in secret and and refusing to comply with the VFOIA. And one evil fruit of this scheme is that it controls the media. If the media is denied access to government records, the media cannot inform the public about important issues. There is nothing more sinister than when the government operates in secrecy.

33. Judges will tell a *pro se* party that the *pro se* party doesn't know the law (and therefore that his argument is dumb) when this is false. Judges will try very hard to make a *pro se* party feel incompetent. Don't back down from your conviction just because the judge criticizes you. He is criticizing you only to frustrate you and to fool you into thinking that you are wrong when you are not wrong. This happened to me many times.

34. When a judge makes a statement such as, "in my opinion," he is obviously not making a statement based on the law. If a judge states, "In my opinion, you are not entitled to a default judgment," for example, that means that you are

entitled to a default judgment because the judge's opinion is irrelevant. If this happens to you, ask the judge to provide you with the rule or law that he is relying upon to come to his opinion. Ask nicely. The fact that you are asking might make him angry. I have heard many judges reply with, "I don't have to give you the statute," which means there most likely isn't one.

35. Judges will block a *pro se* party's cross-examination of a witness and object to the *pro se* party's questions with objections such as, "I am not going to let him answer that because I really don't care if he ate a hamburger before he went to work". This happened to me in City of Fredericksburg (Virginia) Circuit Court case CL11-358 (Judge Gordon F. Willis). Don't back down from the judge's intervention. Explain to the judge that you want the judge to give you a chance to ask your line of questioning before he objects. Keep asking if you need to persuade the judge. Keep asking nicely until he threatens you with contempt of court or sanctions.

36. A judge will fail to rule when a *pro se* party

enters an objection. This happens all the time and this is how judges will block a party's successful appeal. If the judge does not rule, the *pro se* party's objection is not preserved for the record. The *pro se* party needs to say this, "I object on hearsay grounds [or other grounds]...[pause for the judge to rule]...[if the judge does not rule on the objection, the *pro se* party must say this:] Can I get a ruling on my objection please?" Judges will ask the *pro se* party questions that amount to the solicitation of testimony. A *pro se* party is not required to testify and may choose not to testify. When a *pro se* party is making argument in a court of law, he must not answer questions that solicit testimony. For example, the judge might ask, "Let me ask you, where were you on the evening of the 8th of June?" A *pro se* party should respond, "Your honor, I am not testifying. I am acting as legal counsel." The *pro se* party needs to repeat this each time the judge solicits evidence (testimony) from the *pro se* party.

37. Judges will fail to give a *pro se* party an oath

when the *pro se* party attempts to enter his testimony. Therefore, the *pro se* party thinks he is testifying when he is not. Without testimony, there may be no evidence entered to support the *pro se* party's request. Words spoken in a court of law by a *pro se* party are not evidence unless he states that he wants to be put under oath so that he can enter his testimony. A *pro se* party can say something to the judge but unless he is under oath and telling the court that he is giving his testimony, the words said cannot be used by the judge as evidence to support the *pro se* party's request.   However, be careful. Don't jump on a chance to enter testimony because that opens you up to questioning.   You will nearly never successfully defend an accusation by entering testimony. Under such a circumstance, you need only to successfully impeach a key witness or rebut any evidence offered by the other party. If the adverse party makes an accusation but offers no evidence, then you don't need to defend the accusation. You can impeach the witness by asking questions that reveal that his testimony is untrue. But this is a skill that most *pro se* parties don't have. At the same time, it is quite likely your best weapon. I will give you more tips on cross-examination of a witness (for impeachment purposes) in chapter seven.

38. The court reporter a *pro se* party might use in a civil case will suddenly lose the recording of a very important hearing in which the judge admits clearly to violating the *pro se* party's constitutional and human rights. This happened to me in Chesterfield County (Virginia) Circuit Court case CL11-2361. Or the court reporter dramatically increases her fees suddenly (as a result of the adverse party, who is represented by a lawyer, hinting to the court reporter that it has a lot more work for the court reporter than the *pro se* party has). The court reporter is susceptible to bias. A court reporter actually issued me a significant refund without a request to do so after she saw that I had appealed my case in which she was the court reporter to the Supreme Court of the United States. I suspect

that she knew that she could have been caught charging me more for her services than she charged other attorneys.

39. Government employees and public officials will conspire to make the outspoken person look crazy. In 2011, I interviewed with the Virginia state police because I was seeking relief from the crimes committed against me. I had documentary proof of the crimes. I was articulate and intelligent. Yet, at the end of the interview, the state police agent asked me if I heard voices (when nobody was speaking), if I have a history of mental disease in my family, if I wanted him to take me to the hospital, and more. He pursued this line of questioning for about ten minutes. If I had answered "yes" to any question, this agent would have been able to discredit everything I had said on the basis that I am crazy and not credible. He also asked me if I was "anti-American". Had I indicated in any way that I was, he could have used this information to discredit me, to call my motivations into question, and to justify putting me on a list of

people who are anti-American and a threat to society.   There is nearly never a time when a person classified as anti-American is not also classified as a threat to society.

40. Never allow anyone to record your statements unless you have no choice. For example, if you are talking with the state police officer about a crime being committed against you and he asks if he can record the interview, either ignore the question or tell him that he can not.

41. Be aware that a judge could set you up for perjury charges.   Do not testify without the advice of a lawyer.   If you are under oath and testifying, you can refuse to answer questions for a variety of reasons. You could tell the judge that you don't want to testify unless you first have the advice of a lawyer. Under most circumstances, you cannot be forced to testify. But if you do testify, the judge can use every word you say against you. This happened to me in City of Fredericksburg (Virginia) Circuit Court cases CL12-00055 and CL12-00056 which were petitions for writ of mandamus directed to

public officials, the treasurer and sheriff, who refused to comply with the Virginia Freedom of Information Act ("VFOIA"). The treasurer, who had been collecting taxes from me for years and was currently collecting real estate taxes on a house I own, denied my VFOIA request on the false basis that I was not a citizen of Virginia. The deputy treasurer, Brenda Wood, demanded as a condition of responding to my VFOIA request that I provide her with evidence of my physical location. She wanted a lease agreement, driver license, and/or voter registration card despite having documents in her possession that proved that I was currently paying real estate tax to the treasurer. I was under significant threat of bodily harm by public officials and would not provide such evidence. In addition, such evidence is not required to fulfill a VFOIA request. The judge forced me to testify in this civil matter under threat that he would find me in contempt of court if I did not (which he cannot do in a civil matter) to demand that I provide my physical address despite the fact that the record clearly included about more than 60 pages of copies of tax bills paid to the treasurer that established a Virginia address and the fact that the VFOIA does not require a person making a request under the VFOIA to provide evidence of their physical address. I told Judge Bass that I had been threatened and was in danger of bodily harm and was staying in a temporary safe place and he still threatened to find me in contempt of court if I did not testify as to my physical address.   He made no inquiry into my fear of bodily harm. Obviously, Judge Bass was abusing his authority to assist the public officials in their various efforts (which are publicly documented) to find me in a non-public setting and to hurt me.   After I provided the little bit of testimony required, the judge (J. Martin Bass, retired)[10] told counsel for the public officials to investigate my testimony (to

[10] Both former judges Michael C. Allen and J. Martin Bass retired in 2012 and 2013, respectively, and work for the McCammon Group in Richmond, Virginia, as of 8/30/15

investigate my true street address) and to report their findings to him. I objected in writing and orally to Judge Bass' scheme to create an investigation from the bench for the purposes of fabricating a reason to find me in contempt of court or to jail me for perjury. This is a common trick used by many judges to fabricate a reason to find a party in contempt of court and to confine a party to a jail cell to retaliate against that party and/or to force an end to the party's lawsuit since the person cannot pursue his lawsuit from a jail cell. Therefore, obviously, judge Bass forced me to testify only to try to fabricate a reason to charge me with perjury which can result in a jail sentence. In these two cases, it is obvious that Judge Bass was acting solely on behalf of the public officials. One public official, the then-deputy treasurer, Brenda A. Wood (who is now the treasurer) clearly lied under oath. And Judge Bass supported the false testimony. Among other things, Ms. Wood lied and stated under oath that all business licenses issued have the taxpayer ID on them. And for this reason, Ms. Wood testified that she could not provide me with business license information unless I physically stood next to her while she scrolled through business license information on a computer screen and held a piece of paper over the business tax ID. I know that this is untrue for many reasons one of which is the fact that there was and still is a city ordinance that explicitly prohibits business licenses from being issued with the tax ID visible. Further, Ms. Wood testified that she is paid $21.91 per hour and that I would have to pay her hourly wage for a total of about $700 before she could respond to my request under the VFOIA. Ms. Wood testified that only she could perform this ministerial task and that no employee with a lower hourly wage could perform this task for a lower cost. When I filed notices with the court to conduct discovery upon Ms. Wood to, among other things, impeach her testimony, Judge Bass responded by entering a final order in the lawsuit in some secret place at some secret time without my knowledge. When I appealed and filed a written statement of facts, Judge Bass refused to sign it as required. When the Virginia Supreme Court ("VSC") processed my appeal, it falsely stated that there was no record since there was no statement of facts. But there was a statement of facts. I personally saw it in the file at the VSC and the Deputy Clerk, Doug Robelen, confirmed with me that the unsigned statement of facts was in the record. But the statement of facts was not signed by a judge. The VSC had ruled in *Shapiro v. Younkin*, 688 SE 2d 157, 279 Va 256 (2010) that when a trial court judge refuses to sign the statement of facts, the appeal is remanded back to the trial court so that the trial court can sign the statement of facts or otherwise create a record from which the appeal can proceed. But in my appeal VSC 12-1330, the VSC denied my appeal on the false basis that there was no statement of facts in the record. Therefore, Judge Bass and the VSC had unlawfully manipulated the court proceedings to protect the public officials from having to release information subject to the VFOIA. The business license records would show, among other things, that the treasurer and the commissioner of revenue do not require the Fredericksburg Sheriff, employees of the Sheriff's office, and the then-treasurer G.M. Haney, many of whom operated businesses in addition to their public service jobs, to pay business license taxes or property tax for their businesses. Also many of these public service officers and employees are able to circumvent the local zoning laws regarding prohibition of operating a business from a residence. At the same time, the commissioner of revenue, Lois Jacob, went out of her way to assess property tax and business license tax to me that I do not owe. And there was at least once instance in which I paid to the treasurer a tax I did not owe just to get clearance to renew my car registration which the treasurer had blocked. And the treasurer refused to credit to my tax account for my payment. I paid the tax online and authorized an electronic debit from my bank account and had proof that the money came out of my bank account and was credited to the Fredericksburg treasurer. Yet, the treasurer refused to credit my payment to my account and refused to unblock my car registration. This same commissioner of revenue who did not assess taxes to public officials and their employees, Lois Jacob, had knowingly assessed taxes to me for which Ms. Jacob knew I was exempt. And the treasurer, G.M. Haney and his deputy, Brenda A. Wood, refused to refund this unlawfully collected tax without a lawsuit. This is one fine example of how many different government officials and employees worked in harmony to deny a citizen the simple right to records under the VFOIA. This kind of scheme can, and most likely does, happen in every state.

42. Judges will make gross, unintentional, obvious errors and refuse to correct them upon request. This happened to me in City of Frederickburg (Virginia) Circuit Court cases CL11-705 and CL11-706 in which retired judge Gaylord L. Finch Jr. sustained demurrers filed and didn't realize that by sustaining the demurrers, he

ended the lawsuits. After he sustained the demurrers, he started scheduling pre-trial matters. I didn't want to humiliate him. He was retired at that time and had retired from a court that didn't use demurrers (juvenile and domestic relations). But I had to tell him that I knew that he didn't have experience with demurrers and that he meant to say that he denied the demurrers. Upon advising him of this in open court, he seemed weak and literally popped up from his chair and exited the courtroom without ruling on my motion that he correct his statement. Judge Finch violated my constitutional rights when he refused to correct his erroneous statement. Judge Thacher (retired) soon after caused my kidnapping by entering grossly erroneous and false orders in City of Fredericksburg (Virginia) Circuit Court case CL11-358; and I was held for 8 days during which the time to appeal Judge Finch's erroneous order had expired.

43. The court clerk will file a petition for judicial review as a motion in a closed case. This denies the petition for judicial review from being

reviewed. This means that when the clerk of the court makes a decision that is reviewable by the court, the clerk can block your request for review simply by filing your petition for judicial review as a motion in a closed case. This happened to me in Florida Supreme Court cases SC13-2127 (against Florida Chief of Police Gerald M. Bailey) and SC13-2204 (against Governor Rick Scott). I had filed lawsuits against them regarding the fraudulent court activity arising from Orange County Florida circuit court. I will soon be filing a lawsuit in federal court directed to the clerk of the Florida Supreme Court regarding this issue.

44. The judge will use legal terms when the same thing could be said in common terms. He will do this to confuse you. This happened to me in City of Fredericksburg (Virginia) Circuit Court case CL11-358 (Judge Gordon F. Willis). Judge Willis called a typographical error a "scrivener's error", asked if there were any "proffers", and used other legal terms when he knew that I was not a lawyer. It's not common for a *pro se* party to know what these terms mean. But a *pro se* party

would understand if Judge Willis asked for proffers by saying, "Is there anything else that you want to offer in support of your motion? This will be your last opportunity before I rule."

45. This is a trick used by a Pennsylvania state trooper in 2011. He stopped a commercial truck and accused the driver of being overweight. He claimed that the private road the driver was driving on had a maximum weight limit. He gave the driver a ticket that assessed a fine of about $15,000. The driver appeared in court to dispute the charge, and the state trooper who appeared to testify against the driver was not the state trooper who issued the ticket. He therefore had no first-hand knowledge of the facts. Before the hearing began, the state trooper offered to lower the cost of the fine to about $1200 and told the driver that he could pay with a credit card. The driver declined the offer. The driver explained to the judge that the state trooper who stopped his truck and gave him the ticket was not present and explained other relevant facts. The judge dismissed the case.

46. Law enforcement employees and public officials will create fraudulent affidavits. This happened to me. I discovered that an affidavit allegedly dated in June 2010 was filed on April 29, 2011, in Orange County Florida Circuit Court case 2009-CA-037513. This was a problem for many reasons. This affidavit was filed after the final orders were allegedly entered in this lawsuit. There was no proof in the record prior to date of the final orders that gave the court jurisdiction, and this fraudulent affidavit attempted to correct this problem. The documents indicating that a final order had been entered were obviously fraudulent and void. The City of Fredericksburg Sheriff's secretary, Theresa Abel, allegedly notarized this affidavit. But the notary entry was clearly erroneous and did not comply with Virginia law. As one example, the affidavit was dated in June 2010 and the notary stamp showed that the notary's term expired in January 2010. Also, the affiant, William Reyes III, a Fredericksburg Sheriff's deputy, testified under oath that he did not sign the affidavit in the

presence of a notary and that he hadn't written his report that appeared on the affidavit until after the date shown on the affidavit. There is a transcript of his testimony in City of Fredericksburg Circuit Court case CL11-358. I paid for that transcript and have copies of it. The original was filed with the court which most likely lost it. (*See* paragraph 5 on page 68.) Mr Reyes also testified as if he didn't know Theresa Abel personally. He never admitted under oath that she was the Sheriff's secretary, that he saw her nearly every day for the past ten years, that he had lived for at least 10 years in the house next to Ms. Abel's house and that his daughter and her son were childhood friends who frequently played together until his daughter moved away. In addition, the Fredericksburg Sheriff had in his possession two other statements made by then-Sgt Nick Talbert (Sheriff's employee who was superior to Reyes) and Officer David Reilly (Fredericksburg police officer) which directly contradict Mr. Reyes' statement shown on the affidavit. Therefore, the

Sheriff knew at the time that he created the affidavit in question on April 29, 2011, that the words on the affidavit were likely to be false. Yet, he caused them to appear in the form of a statement made under oath; and he knowingly caused the filing of this fraudulent affidavit in a Florida court in Orange County Florida Circuit Court case 2009-CA-037513 which is a fraudulent lawsuit masterminded by a Florida insurance agent's $10,000,000 insurance fraud scheme. This explains why this same Sheriff, Paul Higgs, schemed to kidnap me as referenced on pages 9, 24, 42, and 170 of this book: I discovered in about March 2012 that he created this fraudulent affidavit and I sought relief from it in the courts. And he wanted to silence me. It is not possible to seek relief from a fraudulent affidavit from a coffin or a jail cell.

47. Lawyers will knowingly present fraudulent affidavits as evidence. This happened to me in City of Fredericksburg Circuit Court case CL11-358. The attorney, Turkessa Bynum Rollins, presented the affidavit described in the

immediate paragraph above to the court as evidence. But she removed the Orange County Florida Circuit Court Clerk's time/date stamp which proved that it was not filed with the court until after the date shown on the fraudulent court orders. The transcript of the hearing proves that Ms. Rollins falsely stated to the court that this affidavit was relied upon by the Florida court which falsely implied that this affidavit was filed before the date shown on the fraudulent court orders. If this happens to you, make your objections known and put them on the record. "On the record" only means that you say the words so that the court reporter has them and can provide them at a later time when you order the transcript, your write them down or type them and file them with the clerk of the court, or you write them on the court order.

48. Judges will block your attempt to impeach a witness. When I attempted to impeach Reyes testimony described in paragraph 45 above, Judge Gordon F. Willis intervened excessively to block my ability to impeach him. The transcript

proves this. Judge Willis refused to allow me to ask simple questions, made circular argument (meaningless argument that starts at one point and ends up exactly where the argument began), and refused to let the lawyer for Reyes speak or make her own objections. Since Reyes worked for the Sheriff's office which provides security for Judge Willis, it is obvious that Judge Willis acted solely to control Reyes' testimony. If this happens to you, stand your ground and keep asking your questions. Object to the judge's attempt to block your cross-examination. Make your objections known and for the record.

49. The judge, the clerk or the adverse party will change the style of the lawsuit to commit fraud upon the court. This happened to me many times. It is a significant problem. I will give you one example. I filed a lawsuit against Al Redmer Jr. and the Maryland Insurance Administration ("MIA") in U.S. District Court for Maryland case 1:15-cv-2047. Only Redmer answered the complaint. And when he did, he boldly changed the style of the lawsuit to exclude the MIA as a

named Respondent. I later filed a notice of default against the MIA. And Redmer responded in opposition, by counsel, that the notice of default is not appropriate because Redmer had answered the complaint. But the notice of default was not against Redmer and Redmer knew this. Redmer refused to use the name "Maryland Insurance Administration" at any time and refused to acknowledge that the MIA even exists. Always file a motion with the court to strike court documents that change the style of the lawsuit. Or in the alternative, file a motion asking the court to direct the adverse party to correct all documents which have been filed that do not correctly show the style of the lawsuit. The "style" of a lawsuit is, for example, *Roe v. Wade.* If you file a lawsuit and the defendants are "Mickey Mouse, individually and in his official capacity, and Mickey Mouse Incorporated", then it is incorrect for Mickey Mouse to file an answer to the lawsuit and style his answer to show Mickey Mouse as the only defendant. You don't need to know why the adverse party does this. There are many reasons. Just make sure you correct the problem immediately.

50. People you don't know and have never met will lie about you under oath. The reason why they do this is typically because the other party is paying them for their time or service. This happened to me in City of Fredericksburg (Virginia) Circuit Court case CL11-358 in which Deborah Christensen lied about me. I have the transcript of her testimony. Her lies were obvious. But the judge, Gordon F. Willis, listened to her testimony and gave credence and weight to her testimony against my objections. Her testimony revealed that she notarized her own statement under oath. This invalidates that oath because there is no law in the United States that allows a notary to notarize her own statement. She also testified that she went to my house and knocked on the door, that I opened the door only slightly, that she could not see me, but that it was me who answered the door. As I cross-examined her, it was revealed that she was not the person who knocked on my door and

that she was not present at that time. A different person, a man named Charles, was the true person who knocked on my door at that time. She was testifying falsely because she was giving the false impression that Charles' statement about knocking on my door and speaking to someone through a small opening of the door was her statement. Further, her testimony was without all logic. If I or any person opened my door and Charles could not see the person; it is not possible that Ms. Christensen could state in an affidavit or under oath during the hearing that the person who answered the door was me. But that's exactly what she did. It is very bizarre but strangers who seem to have no interest in the case will readily lie for no apparent reason. But don't forget that if a lawyer pays a witness for his services and the lawyer wins his case, that witness is likely to be in favor with that lawyer and is likely to get more work from that lawyer. The lesson here is: don't trust anyone to tell the truth and prepare for this in advance.

Chapter Five

There are many courts of law in the United States that operate without regard for the U.S. Constitution, the law, or the facts. There is no doubt that these courts are intentionally and totally lawless when they want to be. But they are often not only lawless, but undoubtedly criminal. It would be easier to write about the courts that respected my rights because there are so few of them, in my experience. But before you endeavor to assert your rights, I will share with you the worst courts I experienced. This is important to know because I have given you information that you can use to recognize when a court or its clerk is acting against your rights, intentionally or not, so that you can take steps to try to cure the problems immediately. If you lose your case and later discover that the reason for losing your case is because the court clerk did not file a paper you mailed to the court, you are very unlikely to be able to resolve this after you lose your case. But if you mail a paper to the clerk of the court, check five days later to see if it was received. And if it was not, take steps immediately to remedy the problem. This information can be used to assess your situation in any court of law. But this information below will explore my personal experience to help you recognize some tricks the courts and their clerks play to deny you your rights.

The first thing you must understand is that the clerk is nearly never an impartial record keeper. Her only role is to be an impartial record keeper. But that is nearly never the case. Most often, the clerk is eager to sabotage your lawsuit with a variety of tricks. Therefore, you must get a file-stamped copy of every document you file with the court. Make sure that the file stamp is very clear so that it can be easily seen on the scanned version of the document (since I expect you to scan each document and save it in electronic format).

The worst courts in my experience are as follows:

Florida state and federal courts

Virginia state and federal courts

Texas district and federal courts

Illinois federal courts

District of Columbia federal courts

Wyoming state and federal courts

Florida state and federal courts

Florida state and federal courts are hopelessly lawless and criminal in my experience. This does not mean that you should abandon all hope. It only means that you should avoid Florida unless you have inside connections with the courts, clerks, and judges. Without such connections, you can expect to have to exert excessive effort just to get even an ounce of justice. You may get no justice.

Orange County Florida Circuit Court has been the source of many problems for many people during recent years; from about 2001 to 2013. One reason for this is that the clerk of this court, Lydia Gardner, instituted an anonymous drop-box filing system by which people could anonymously drop court orders in the box for filing. This is shocking because a court order should go directly from the judge's hand to the clerk's hand to make sure that the security and integrity of the court order is retained. But Ms. Gardner's anonymous drop-box resulted in many criminals taking advantage of this lack of security. Many convicted murders filed their own early-release orders this way. The Florida Department of

Corrections relied upon these fraudulent orders and unknowingly released many convicted murders. The Florida Senate conducted a judiciary committee meeting in November 2013 to address this problem.[11] The Florida Senate decided to investigate about 7800 criminal court orders as a result. But they ignored the fact that this problem involved civil court orders as well and ignored my written request that they investigate my Orange County Florida Court case 2009-CA-037513.

The Eleventh Circuit court of appeals is the

[11] During this Florida Senate committee meeting, it was publicly revealed that the former Orange County Florida Circuit Court ("OCFCC") clerk, Ms. Lydia Gardner, who had been the clerk of this OCFCC since 2001, had pioneered a drop-box filing system whereby anyone could anonymously drop court orders to be filed with the clerk of the OCFCC. Ms. Gardner died in May 2013. According to the then Commissioner of the Florida Department of Law Enforcement, Gerald M Bailey, "Due to lack of good audit trails we are still trying to figure out how the documents got to the Clerks [sic] office." *See* p. 100 of Florida Senate Meeting Packet from November 2013 located at: http://www.flsenate.gov/PublishedContent/Committees/2012-2014/ACJ/MeetingRecords/MeetingPacket_2365.pdf, last accessed 8/30/15.

appellate court for the U.S. District Courts in Florida. And it has fully supported the illogical and erroneous court orders arising from U.S. District Court for the Middle District of Florida case 5:14-cv-00410.

Virginia state and federal courts

Let me start with positive comments because you need to know when you are in the present of an impartial judge who follows the law.

The best judges I have seen in Virginia are Judges John Scott (who passed away in 2008 and was replaced by Judge Gordon F. Willis), John R. Stevens of the Fredericksburg General District Court and Donald P. McDonough (retired), former Chief Judge of Fairfax County General District Court. Judge Scott was the chief judge of the City of Fredericksburg Circuit Court who was legally blind and brilliant and whose rulings lined up well with the law. Judge Stevens digs in to resolve issues. He doesn't seem too quick to throw the book at people. He seems fair. One time there was a dispute between two women over a man in whom both had a love interest. He had the two women come forward together and he seemed to basically walk them through resolution, gently suggesting that this man might not be worth spending time in jail. This discussion lasted for maybe five minutes. He discussed ways they could avoid each other by driving a different way to work, for example. The two women left the courtroom in peace with charges dismissed but with the threat that they better not appear in Judge Stevens' court again; otherwise, there would be serious consequences. Judge Stevens has not always been fair to me. His fair treatment ended after I began a dispute against the city treasurer, G.M. Haney, because he refused to refund about $4000 in taxes I paid that were unlawfully assessed by the commissioner of revenue, Lois Jacob.

Judge Stevens was once the Chief Judge of the 15th Judicial District for the general district courts. Judge Ricardo Rigual is the current Chief Judge. And quite frankly, he missed his calling as a model. He is Hollywood handsome. This is an obvious problem for women who can't focus well enough to speak thoughtfully when he is the judge. That is no exaggeration. And even the court personnel have been known to be giddy when they hear defendants say something like, "That is one good looking man!" while cheerfully paying their court fines and costs. This is important because it demonstrates that female witnesses in his courtroom are quite likely to struggle with their testimony. There is no jury impaneled in Virginia general district courts which adjudicate traffic citations and small disputes. But this brings about a very good point. The more well-groomed and attractive you are, the better chances you will have in court because people give attractive people more time, consideration, and leniency. (It's a statistic. Don't shoot the messenger.)

Judge McDonough explains to the courtroom and *pro se* parties the procedures. For example, he will tell a *pro se* party that he can make an opening argument but that it is not evidence and that the *pro se* party, if he plans to enter testimony that is similar or the same as his opening argument, will need to repeat the same words under oath when he gives his testimony.   I once saw a *pro se* party who was so close to winning his case.   And Judge McDonough needed only that the party prove his damages (such as a receipt for the repair of his car). But Judge McDonough did not tell the *pro se* party this. Instead, he said at least three times, "Is there anything else that you want to present as evidence before I rule?" Judge McDonough said, "Are you sure because I am ready to rule" And the *pro se* party said that he was sure. Then you could hear many people in the courtroom moan with pity for the *pro se* party when the judge ruled against him. Even the bailiff, a portly blond, friendly woman,who laughed at Judge McDonough's jokes, shrugged her shoulders in an expression of "ah, shucks" when the judge ruled against him. But Judge McDonough is the only judge I have seen who explains basic courtroom procedures to *pro se* parties. He also explained the origin of sequestering witnesses.

Here is one example of an unethical Virginia lawyer and a good reason why you must always be prepared to face a lion when you face a lawyer (and judges are lawyers): K Vanessa Rodriguez, of Fairfax, Virginia. She was the lawyer in a 2012 Fairfax General District Court case which falsely accused the defendant of stealing documents from the plaintiff. I know first hand that the truth is that the plaintiff had not paid the defendant for the documents and the documents were never in the plaintiff's possession because of his failure to pay for them. I got involved to try to help resolve the dispute after the plaintiff obtained a default judgment (by filing a lawsuit in a court far away from the defendant's resident address). The defendant and I went to Ms. Rodriguez's office to collect the money the plaintiff owed, and the defendant agreed to give the plaintiff the documents in exchange. After the transaction was finished (which got hostile), I asked Ms. Rodriguez to provide the defendant with a written notice of satisfaction of judgment. She refused to provide it on the basis that she didn't know who was going to pay her legal fees to draft the document. I explained that it was unethical to demand that the defendant pay her legal fees only to draw up a document that truthfully disclosed that the plaintiff received the full demands of the default judgment. She claimed that her legal fees for the lawsuit had not been paid. I began videotaping her statements with a cell phone and I made no secret about it. Suddenly, a man burst through the office door and pushed me and tried to take my cell phone from my hand and told me that I can't videotape. Ms. Rodriguez yelled at him to stop and she literally pushed him out of the office. She immediately typed up a notice of satisfaction of judgment and we left her office. I have this incident on videotape and there were two other witnesses with me. But this is just one example of the ways a lawyer will try to take advantage of a party (making untrue statements in a complaint and filing a complaint in a court far away from the defendant) and of a party's ignorance of the law and procedures. Had Ms. Rodriguez refused to provide a notice of satisfaction of judgment after the defendant gave the plaintiff the documents, the plaintiff would have the documents but a judgment would still exist that falsely established on the court record that the plaintiff had not received the documents.

Most judges, who are lawyers, are cut from the same cloth as Ms. Rodriguez.

In my personal experience, Virginia state judges have created fraudulent court documents, conspired with attorneys to create fraudulent documents, and boldly acted without regard for the law. A lawsuit I filed in 2015 in the U.S. District Court for the Eastern District of Virginia in Richmond case number 3:15-cv-00206 describes the fraudulent and criminal abuse of the courts by Virginia state judges which includes the criminal actions of Judge Steven Colin McCallum who has abused his authority to steal a house I own in Virginia in Chesterfield County Circuit Court case CL14-1255. I filed this lawsuit in March 2015 and included an emergency motion for a temporary restraining order which the district court ignored for more than four months before it dismissed the lawsuit on erroneous grounds.

I had a similar experience in another lawsuit I filed in July 2015 in the U.S. District Court for the Eastern District of Virginia in Alexandria, case number 1:15-cv-00903, which describes the same fraudulent and criminal abuse of the courts by Virginia state judges which includes the criminal actions of judge Steven Colin McCallum who has abused his authority to steal a house I own in Virginia in Chesterfield County Circuit Court case CL14-1255. I filed this lawsuit in July 2015 and included an emergency motion for a temporary restraining order which the district court ignored for six weeks despite the fact that I filed a petition for a writ of mandamus with the Fourth Circuit Court of Appeals asking it to direct the district court to do its job and rule on my emergency motion.

So obviously, the Virginia state courts abuse their authority to commit crimes and at least two of the Virginia federal courts support them.

I have filed many complaints with the Virginia House and Senate members of the Courts of Justice

Committee. They elect and re-elect Virginia state judges. And Virginia judges have only acted with increased malice toward me.

The U.S. District Courts in the Western district of Virginia seem to be more compliant with the U.S. Constitution than the Eastern District.

Texas district and federal courts

My experience with the Texas state courts is similar to my experience in the Virginia state courts. *See* Travis County (Texas) District Court cases D-1-GN-13-002576 and D-1-GN-13-001957. But bear in mind that the clerk of this court has inserted fraudulent documents into these case records and has omitted relevant documents from these case records. If you want correct documents from these lawsuits, you can order them from me. *See* page 1. Lawsuits in federal court are pending against two clerks of this court in U.S. District Court for the Western District of Texas case numbers 1:2014-cv-00510 and 1:2015-cv-00405. Problems with these lawsuits filed in Travis County (Texas) District Court against the Texas Department of Insurance were created by the clerks of this court, Amalia Rodriguez-Mendoza (retired) and Velva L. Price. They both entered or caused the entry of false and fraudulent documents into the records and refused to perform ministerial duties. In addition, many employees of this court lied to me on the telephone and took many steps to make it impossible for me to move my lawsuits forward. On April 15, 2015, I requested that Ms. Price provide me with the clerk's records under the Texas open records act (Texas Gov't Code Section 522 et seq.). Ms. Price ignored my request. It is very difficult to manage your lawsuit if fraudulent documents are being secretly entered by the clerk of the court. My lawsuits in this Texas court were filed in 2013, more than two years ago. And they have been stalled by the tricks of the clerks of this court. The federal courts have entered grossly erroneous orders that function to support the criminal actions of the clerks of this court. Willful violations of a a person's constitutional rights (which include, among other things Due Process) are a crime under the U.S. Code Title 18 Sections 241 and 242.

Illinois federal courts

My experience with the U.S. District Court in Springfield, Illinois is one of my worst experiences with any court. I have received court orders from a staff attorney who has no authority to enter rulings. I have received unsigned, anonymous orders.

Judge Richard Mills entered grossly erroneous orders. As one example, one order stated that I have $1845 in monthly income and $2145 in monthly expenses. Therefore, Judge Mills asserted that I have enough funds to pay the $500 filing fee. This is totally illogical. When I asked for relief from this erroneous order, Judge Mills classified my request as frivolous. Judge Mills also threatened to sanction me if I filed any additional papers with the court alleging my poverty. This means that Judge Mills denied my request to proceed without prepayment of fees despite the fact that public records prove that other litigants with greater income were allowed to proceed without prepayment of fees and then threatened to sanction me only because I sought relief from the court's abuse of authority.

Appealing to the Seventh Circuit Court of Appeals was fruitless because Judge Mills had entered an order stating that my claim of poverty is frivolous.

There is only one or two other courts in the United States that fabricated reasons to deny my request to proceed without prepayment of fees. And one such denial was overturned on appeal. The other is pending.

Wyoming Federal Court

If you want to read some truly ridiculous court orders and how I responded to them, order the documents from me or from www.Pacer.gov for U.S. District Court case 2:14-cv-00089-NDF. It will be cheaper to order them from me because Pacer.gov charges 10 cents per page downloaded; whereas, you can order the documents from me for $9.95. *See* page 1.

As one example, the U.S. Magistrate judge falsely stated in an order entered on December 30, 2014, at docket entry 47, on page 2, "Respondent claims it has not been served through a registered agent, and therefore has not and cannot waive service." This is a total fabrication by the court. And this was obvious evidence that the court was coaching the respondent to assert the defense of insufficient process (which it never did).

Chapter Six

This chapter discusses the administrative tasks.

First, don't underestimate yourself. If you study, learn the rules and the laws; you can outwit a lawyer. Sometimes you can outwit him because he might underestimate you and be unprepared. Sometimes you can outwit him just because he might be consumed with a big trial. Or maybe you are just really smart. But I think most lawyers are mediocre at best. There are some good ones out there. And the good ones are the ones who know the law, work within the law, and know the law well enough to make it work in their favor. The good ones don't lie because they know they can outwit most other lawyers. The best lawyers do not usually work for the government (except in very top positions). If the lawyer for the adverse party is a government employee, I would classify him as less than mediocre. Don't let the fact that the other side is represented by a lawyer intimidate you.

I recommend sitting in the court where you will be presenting your case when the court is in session to get a feel for the judge and the process. You might need to sit there for three or four days, about two to four hours each day.   Take notes. Observe.

Always use as few words as possible and only state the facts and the law.   I repeat this because it is worth repeating. Never, never, never talk or email or otherwise communicate with any lawyer unless you are filing that communication with the court or you paying him to represent you. Never, never! If you must email something that is not filed with the court, stick only to the facts such as: the opposing attorney emails you and asks you if you are available for a deposition on September 20, 2015. Reply only with "yes" or "no". Don't explain why the answer is "yes" or "no". If the answer is "no", include in your reply dates when you are available. I promise you, if you break this rule, you are quite likely to lose your lawsuit only because you broke this rule. Remember, a judge is a lawyer. Never, never! And if you get a snide remark from a lawyer, ignore it. He is only trying to provoke you.

To find which federal court you in which you need to file your petition or complaint, go to: http://www.uscourts.gov/court-locator.

Every state has its own judicial system. Research your state's court system to determine in which court you need to file your lawsuit.

There is a wealth of information on the Internet and in libraries on the common terminology used by courts. Learn these terms.

Learn the state or federal rules of civil procedure, the court's local rules, the state or local administrative rules (not all courts have these), and state and federal appellate rules. You can find these on the Internet. Make sure you are reading the most recently-published versions.

If applicable, always use the Freedom of Information Act to get evidence in support of your case. In Virginia, many, many requests that I have made under the Virginia Freedom of Information Act ("VFOIA") were unlawfully ignored or denied. In addition, Virginia is the only state in the United States that will deny a VFOIA request if you are not a resident of Virginia even if Virginia collects information about you for child support purposes, for example. A trick I have seen used by many Virginia agencies is as follows: the requester gets a response to a VFOIA request which advises the requester that the agency has the information requested and that the requester can travel to their office to retrieve it. So, if the office from which the requester makes the request is far away, requiring him to travel extensively to receive the information is the same as denying the information. The government is required to freely provide the information and is prohibited from creating obstacles to obtain the information. In fact, it is much easier for the government to email the requester the information. It saves substantially on the cost of responding to a VFOIA request. But if the government wants to unlawfully block your request without explicitly telling you that your request is being unlawfully blocked, it will use tricks such as this to block you request. Sarah Kirkpatrick of the City of Fredericksburg Virginia Police Department used this trick in August 2015 with someone I know. And her predecessor, Natatia Bledsoe used a different trick in July 2012 and refused to respond to a VFOIA request I made as follows: "This information will not be provided to you until you are served on an outstanding capias issued by the Fredericksburg Circuit Court." (This relates to the many attempts by Virginia public officials to create fraudulent court documents to kidnap me.) The VFOIA does not permit such a denial. When the government uses trickery to deny your request for documents, this establishes that the government is engaged in activity it wants to keep secret and has abandoned the U.S. Constitution (which establishes that the citizens are the master and the government is the servant). This kind of block by the government is a crime against the citizens and has happened to me on a regular basis when I have made similar requests of government agencies in many states. The government will not hesitate to violate the law to block your pursuit of justice. So, this is not always going to bear fruit after you file your lawsuit. Therefore, try to make your requests under the Freedom of Information Act before you file your lawsuit.

The clerk of the court is often called the "clerk" or "register". This person is the keeper of the records.

Many clerk websites have information about how to proceed in your lawsuit *pro se.* Review that information but the information provided will not fully equip you to represent yourself.

It is not recommended that you represent yourself unless you are fully committed to doing your research and of being able to base all your arguments on the facts and the law. Expressing your feelings and making any attempt to provoke a judge's sympathy is most likely a waste of energy and absolutely takes away from your credibility in the eyes of the court.

If the court does not have electronic filing or if you are denied access to electronic filing: every time you file a document, bring a copy of the first page of the document with you and ask the clerk to time/date stamp it for your records. If you are filing by mail, include this copy in the envelope, write on it "CLERK, PLEASE STAMP AND RETURN TO ME", and enclose a self-addressed, stamped envelope.

One time I was speaking before the Supreme Court of Virginia on an appeal that I had filed, and I noticed former Justice Leroy R. Hassell Sr.[12]   rolled his eyes as I approached the podium. Many, if not most, judges and lawyers, dread having to deal with a *pro se* party. I believe it is because *pro se* parties don't know the laws or the rules. I subsequently discovered that Justice Hassell quite likely rolled his eyes for many reasons, including the fact that the judge, Michael C. Allen (retired) of Chesterfield County, Virginia, had manipulated the court file in such a way as to make my appeal impossible. After that experience, I made sure to bring a court reporter to every court appearance so that she could document the judge's violations of the rules and laws on the record. This won't solve the problem completely. But hopefully, the judge will be mindful that he is being recorded and act civilly. And as a result, I will have a better record upon which the appellate court can rely. In Virginia, the Virginia Supreme Court will look only at the final appealable order to determine whether or not an appeal can succeed.   Therefore, if the final

[12] He passed away in 2011. His son, Leroy R. Hassell Jr., has a long criminal history and was sentenced to six years in prison soon after his father died.

order does not explicitly show objections to the trial court's ruling, the Supreme Court of Virginia will determine that there are no reversible errors. Therefore, if the trial court judge unlawfully replaces a final appealable order which shows your signature and your objections with a final appealable order that dispenses with your endorsement and does not show your objections[13], the Supreme Court of Virginia will deny your petition.

One time I had a court reporter present and the judge, Thomas L. Murphey (retired in 2011)[14], talked

---

[13] This happened to me in Chesterfield County (Virginia) Circuit Court case CL11-2361 over which retired judge Michael C. Allen was presiding. I discovered this fraudulent second final order and made my objections part of the record and addressed this problem in my petition for appeal. But the Supreme Court of Virginia denied my appeal anyway. As you probably realize by now, the Virginia judicial system will not hesitate to act without regard for the law in retaliation against a person like me who uncovers unlawful acts by judges and then who seeks relief from such unlawful acts.

[14] Judge Thomas L. Murphey's father was Douglas Woodfin Murphey, a judge of the 12th Judicial Circuit Court of Virginia. The elder Murphey passed away in 1995.

excessively about his erroneous understanding of bankruptcy law. This was in Chesterfield County General District Court V0915424 in 2009. Bankruptcy law was irrelevant. But this can be a problem because you have to pay the court reporter for her time to listen to the judge's irrelevant ramblings and your cost of ordering the full transcript can skyrocket just because the judge kept talking about irrelevant topics. But you can always order only part of the transcript such as the pages that contain the judge's ruling, for example.

I once read a brief filed in the Supreme Court of the United States by a woman from California who protested being sent to jail for 12 months for direct contempt of court. She was so intelligent. She filed her brief from the jail and cited laws based only on her memory. But her petition was very poorly written primarily because she was very emotional and often used bold type and underline only for emphasis. Of course she was emotional. Her life was turned upside down because she was in jail. But don't represent yourself if you can't restrain your emotion. Bold type face and underline, for the purpose of emphasis, annoys lawyers and judges. Use bold and underline only if trying to draw attention to, for example, text in a document that amends another document; as a courtesy to help the reader to know the only change between the two documents.

Typically, your lawsuit must be personally served upon the adverse party. The definition of "personally served" is typically set forth in the state law. The adverse party can also typically be served by "substitute service". You should familiarize yourself with the state law. I used the word "typically" repeatedly because you must learn your state law. Service upon adverse parties in federal courts is typically based on state law. Review the federal rules of civil procedure at http://www.law.cornell.edu. This often requires the "clerk" to create a "summons" or "citation". This "summons" or "citation" advises the adverse party that a lawsuit was filed against him and informs him of the steps he needs to take to avoid default. Attached to this summons or citation is a copy of your complaint. Typically, you need to provide the "clerk" or "register" with one copy of your complaint to be attached to each summons if you are proceeding without prepayment of fees.   Sometimes, you pay the clerk the cost of serving the adverse party with the summons and the complaint (typically includes the cost to produce the summons and cost of paying the person who serves the adverse party) and the clerk gives the summons (with the complaint attached) to the local "sheriff" or "constable" (used in Texas) or "U.S. Marshal" (if in federal court).   Otherwise, once the clerk produces the summons, you will get that summons from the clerk and attach a copy of your complaint to it and take it to a private process server or "sheriff", "constable", or "U.S. Marshal". If you know someone who is over age 18 who might be willing to serve the adverse party for you for less than the cost of the "sheriff", "constable" or "U.S. Marshal"; you typically have no restrictions on who you use to serve the adverse party as long as you meet the state law requirements which typically require only that the person be over age 18 and a disinterested party.   Typically, the person serving the lawsuit will want you to provide the appropriate "proof of service" form for him to complete after he has served the adverse party.   The U.S. Marshal form is form number USM285.   The state forms are different. Also, you can create your own "proof of service" form which is included in the documents available for purchase. *See* page 1.   Make sure that this "proof of service" is filed with the court as soon as possible. Most courts give you 90 days or less to serve the adverse party. If you can't serve the adverse party within the established deadline, you must typically ask the court for an extension of time, explain that you have attempted to serve the person but can't find the person, and request the court to produce an "alias" summons which is the same as the first summons but produced after the first summons is produced.   Also, if you find out that the address on the summons is not correct, you need to get an "alias" summons that shows the correct address.   If there are any problems with the "proof of service", you may need to have the adverse party served a second time.

Always know the rules of civil procedure, the local rules, the administrative rules, the statutory laws, the rules of appellate procedures, and the standing rules. Not all courts have published local rules, administrative rules, or standing rules. Most courts will have all their local rules, administrative rules, and standing rules published on their websites. In August 2015, I discovered that the Travis County (Texas) District Court published outdated local rules on its website. The version on its website was from 2011. But the most recent version of local rules was updated in 2014. Be very careful that the rules you are relying upon are the most updated version.

Nearly all federal courts have local rules and standing rules. Local rules often address issues such as the procedure for scheduling hearings and how many copies, if any, need to be mailed to the court. As one of the many examples I could offer, Florida Supreme Court rules require you to email your brief in Microsoft Word format and mail hard copies.

Be careful to notice if any rule requires you to make a statement under oath or requires you to provide a notarized statement that contains your oath. A "jurat" typically involves a notarized statement. Learn the legal terms so that you know whether or not you need your statement notarized. Any statement under oath should not include the phrase, "to the best of my knowledge" or anything similar that means that you are not 100% certain about your statements. Your oath should state something to the effect of: "the foregoing statements are true and correct and made under penalty of perjury on this [day] day of _____[month], _____[year]"

Second, always research your options for electronic filing. You may need to seek permission to file electronically. Most federal courts require lawyers to file electronically and allow *pro se* parties to seek permission to file electronically. Some state courts require electronic filing.

Third, use the court's forms only if they fully meet your needs. Most forms are available online on the clerk's website. Some forms are so basic that you should most likely use them in lieu of typing our own form.

Fourth, always request to proceed *in forma pauperis* ("IFP") if you qualify. If this request is granted, the court will waive costs such as the filing fee, the fee for the summons issuance, the fee for service by the sheriff, transcripts, and more. If you are not sure whether or not you qualify, don't ask the clerk. Just file your request with the court. As with everything you do, never lie. At the same time, be very careful to complete the form correctly. For example, many courts do not ask you if you own a home. They ask only about your income. Therefore, don't volunteer that you own a home. In reporting your income, be mindful to determine whether or not the form asks for your gross income or net income. Also, be mindful not to get too personal on any request to proceed *in forma pauperis*. Many IFP forms will ask if you receive government assistance. If you do, just indicate that you do. Don't provide details about your personal life. For example, if you are disabled and receive disability benefits, don't get into detail about your disability.

Ask to appear at any hearings by telephone if you prefer to appear by telephone. Ask for any accommodations you might need for your hearing such as conference call equipment. In other words, the courtroom where your hearing will take place must be equipped with conference call equipment. If you ask to appear by telephone, make sure you take steps to request that the court be equipped as necessary.

If you need an interpreter, make this request two weeks in advance or more. You should ask for an interpreter even if you think you have a good working knowledge of English when English is not your first language.

Always ask for a trial by jury when you file your complaint. You can always change your mind later. But you often cannot request a jury trial after you file your complaint.

An order from a court is never final. You can typically ask for a new hearing or ask that the order be vacated.

Always meet the deadlines. Every court defines "filed" differently. Some define "filed" as when a document was mailed. Some courts define "filed"as a ten-day time frame after the deadline if filing by mail. In other words, the court gives a document ten days to be received.

Always have a court reporter if one is not provided. If you are appearing by telephone, record the telephone call.

Never, never, never, never, never, never discuss your lawsuit with the opposing side, with opposing counsel, or anybody else. This is quite likely the biggest mistake you could make. Every word you say or type will be twisted against you. Never email the adverse party or opposing counsel unless you are only emailing a court document that you filed.

Don't be naive and think that the truth will prevail. I say this because the lawyers conspire with the judges all the time. So, the truth alone is probably not going to win your lawsuit because the truth is whatever the judge believes, wants to believe, or pretends to believe. In addition, most lawyers I have encountered will readily file fraudulent documents and make false and fraudulent statements to the court. False argument in a court document is not a legal strategy. It is a violation of the professional standards of every lawyer in every court. However, it is not likely that any lawyer will be willing to allow the truth to pass through his mind or his lips. Many prosecutors convict innocent people by fabricating an unproven theory and basing their prosecution solely on this theory. Damien Echols is just one example of a person sentenced to death based only on a prosecutor's theory. Damien Echols was sentenced to three death sentences in Arkansas. Go to www.DamienEchols.com

In my personal experience, Turkessa Bynum Rollins (Virginia lawyer) and Kenneth D. Morse (Florida lawyer) both knowingly filed false and fraudulent documents in many Florida and Virginia courts to perpetuate a $10,000,000 insurance fraud scheme on behalf of Lester Kalmanson Agency, Inc., and Mitchel Kalmanson in Orange County Florida Circuit court case 2009-CA-037513, and in City of Fredericksburg (Virginia) Circuit Court case CL11-358. And every single judge involved in these lawsuits entered court orders without jurisdiction, that were obtained by fraud upon the court, that were obtained by extrinsic fraud, and more. At least three or four judges knowingly assisted Kenneth D. Morse and Turkessa Bynum Rollins with the criminal scheme. And Kenneth D. Morse was able to criminally use the Florida court to commit the insurance fraud scheme with the help of the clerk of court, Lydia Gardner, who established a filing system by which any person could anonymously file fraudulent court orders. *See* Footnote 11 on p. 121

Chapter Seven

This chapter will give you some good ideas on how to impeach a witness or otherwise nullify his testimony. This is done during a deposition, hearing, and/or trial. I will give you two real-life examples. Don't forget that you have a much better chance of winning your lawsuit if you can make the witnesses for the other side admit that they are lying, that they don't know the truth, that they don't know the facts, that they are not sure of their testimony, that they were coerced to testify, etc.

Cross-examining witnesses is a skill you should practice.

Never ask a question to which the answer will not help you.

Start out by laying the foundation with the witness. Get the witness to provide his name and address. Ask his age, where he went to high school, where he went to college, where he was born, etc. This is important because you want to know where he has lived in the past. There may be public records in a different city or state that establish that he is dishonest. If you can find such evidence, you can use it to call his character into question.

When laying this foundation, ask the witness to describe his daily activities, for example. If he tells you that he is a journalist, ask him to describe what he does on a daily basis. So, for example, if he states that he writes magazine articles for a major news outlet and he later acts like he doesn't know the answer to a simple question; you can ask something like, "Earlier you stated that you write articles for a major magazine, correct?" [Wait for answer.] "So, is it fair to say that you are educated? And you went to college?" [Wait for answer]   "So, when I asked you the approximate distance between you and the car and you said, 'I don't know,' is that because you don't know how to measure distance?" [Wait for answer] If he answers that he is just not good with measuring distances without a tape measure, you can say, "How many steps would you have to take to walk to the car?" [Wait for answer] If he says that he doesn't know; ask, "Can you give me an estimate?" If he says that he really doesn't know, and it is important to establish this point, ask, "Was it closer or farther than the distance between the front door of your house to your mailbox [assuming you already researched him and know that he lives in a house with a mailbox at the street]?" If he says that he doesn't know, you ask, "Do you ever walk to your mailbox?" If he answers yes, then ask, "How often do you walk to your mailbox?" If he says "everyday", then ask, "And you have no idea the distance between your front door and your mailbox?" [Wait for answer] If he says that he does not know the distance, then you can ask "You previously testified that you are educated, so I assume you know how many inches one foot is, correct?"   [Wait for answer] "How far would you say that you are sitting from the judge?" [Wait for answer] At this point, he should give you an idea of the distance between him and the judge. At this point you can ask, "You were able to estimate the distance between you and the judge but not able to estimate the distance between you and the car. Is that because you weren't there or your don't remember?" [Wait for answer] At this point, he will hopefully say something that calls into question his recollection of the event. Therefore, if he subsequently makes a statement of certainty about the same event, you can ask, "But I thought you told me earlier that you could not recall the distance between you and the car. And now you seem so certain of the event. So, which is true? You don't have a good recollection or you do have a good recollection?" At this point, he might get nervous and say something contradictory. You can ask, "Do you get easily confused?" And maybe he will say "yes" or "sometimes" or that he is not clear about the questions you are asking (which shows confusion). And if he does, his whole testimony could be called into question because he just admitted to being confused about a simple question such as the distance between him and the car.

When you ask "foundation" questions, these questions are easy and the witness will be relaxed and hopefully answer easily. Be friendly. Thank the witness up front for his time and tell him that you will not take long. Keep a calm voice.

In a deposition, you have a lot of freedom to ask questions. But during a trial or hearing, you will be restricted by the rules of evidence. Learn those rules (such as the "hearsay" rule). You can easily win your lawsuit with a good cross-examination. So, spend as much time as you need to learn the rules of evidence which are typically established on a state-wide or nation-wide basis. The local courts don't typically have their own separate rules of evidence and use the rules published by the supreme court of that state. The federal rules of evidence are located at http://www.law.cornell.edu

In my deposition of Jacqueline Colon of Lehigh Acres, Florida in 2013, it ended with her screaming and crying and running out of the room while I was cross-examining her. She cried and yelled to the opposing counsel, a government lawyer, "I can't do this anymore. I don't care if you put me in jail. I just can't do this." [paraphrasing] Well, this called her entire testimony into question because she just admitted to having been coerced under the threat of criminal prosecution. And the question I asked her was completely non-threatening. I researched her in advance and found out that she was married to a sex offender. I began asking questions to try to get her to admit that she had found no fault in me or my services. And she admitted that she was testifying only because she was asked. I asked her if she believed in forgiveness (even though she never accused me of causing her any harm). And she wiggled around on the reply. I then asked something to the effect of, "Your husband is a registered sex offender.   And maybe he was falsely accused. I know this happened many years ago. And the courts aren't always fair..." She interrupted and screamed, "What does my husband have to do with this?!!" She ran out of the room crying and whaling and made some statements as described above that established that her testimony was coerced under threat of criminal prosecution.[15]

[15] I researched the witness as much as I could prior to the deposition. There were many Jacqueline Colon's in Florida. The deposition was conducted by conference call.   But among the information I found about her was a blog in Yahoo!® in which she voluntarily posted an admission to feeling like a drug addict at times. This is great information to use against a witness.

Notwithstanding, the Florida Department of Financial Services ("FDFS") still used part of her deposition in a hearing against me in 2013 in which I was denied my right to attend. Therefore, I was not allowed to object at the hearing to the admission of this deposition transcript. But even if I was present, the administrative judge was one of those public officials acting without regard for the U.S. Constitution or the law. So my presence would not have made a difference in that hearing only because the administrative judge had no intention of being impartial. The record in Florida Division of Administrative Hearings case 12-3622PL proves that the FDFS abused its authority solely to attempt to kidnap me (force me to travel to Florida to defend the fraudulent administrative action) for the sole purpose of attempting to enforce the fraudulent court orders arising from Orange County Florida Circuit Court case 2009-CA-037513.

Chapter Eight

This chapter will discuss options when your judge is acting without regard for the law or the rules or when or if you lose your case.

There are deadlines for doing nearly everything related to the court. Check your deadlines and adhere to them. They are found in the rules and the law.

You can file a motion with the court to vacate or to set aside its ruling.

You can also appeal.

You can also collaterally attack the judgment based on fraud, deceit, clerical error, etc.

File complaints against the judge. The instructions for federal judges are located at 28 U.S.C. §§ 351-364. The instructions for state judges is easily found on the Internet. Bear in mind that your complaint is being filed with a judge (who is a lawyer) against another judge (who is a lawyer). This method is unlikely to bear fruit. But do it anyway. You never know until you try.

For federal judges, file a one-page petition with each member of the U.S. House of Representatives Judiciary Committee asking that the judge in question be impeached. Be specific as to why you believe impeachment is appropriate. You can get the mailing addresses and fax numbers of each House member on the Internet. I also provide this information if you order the documents as described on the inside cover of this book. Keep your petition under one page in length.

File a petition seeking relief for violations of your human rights with the Organization of American States. (*See* http://www.oas.org) They will take about one or two years to acknowledge your petition and about five years to let you know whether or not they will review your petition. But do it anyway. Once they begin their review, it can take another year or more to get a final ruling.

Write a book sharing your experience with others

Chapter Nine

This chapter will give you real-life examples of gross violations of the U.S. Constitution by government officials so that you can be better equipped to recognize such government actions and try to protect yourself.

In 2012, in Florida, a man named TW owned a dog that bit someone. The local law enforcement charged him with a felony crime for this accident and told him that the charge would be dropped if he euthanized his dog. This violates the U.S. Constitution. I won't explain all the reasons why but to put it simply, it violates the Due Process clause whereby the government takes a citizen's property (the dog) by force.

I helped TW obtain liability insurance so that he could avoid having to euthanize his dog. The local city attorney told TW that he would not accept the insurance policy because I was not licensed to transact insurance in Florida. But I was licensed to transact insurance in Florida. I searched the Florida Department of Financial Services ("FDFS") online licensee look-up system for my license status, and it returned no results. My name and information had been deleted from the FDFS licensee database for the sole purpose of giving the city attorney justification to reject TW's insurance. However, the law in Florida, and all states, establishes that an insurance policy remains in force even if the insurance agent dies or is no longer working for the insurance company or is no longer licensed to transact insurance, etc. But the city attorney, knowing that he could not reject the insurance policy on this basis, rejected it anyway. And what you must understand is that an insurance policy will not prevent a future injury. So, requiring a dog owner to purchase insurance is almost entirely nothing but a financial obstacle imposed upon the dog owner. If the city attorney truly wanted to protect the public, he would only require the dog owner to physically restrain the dog at all times. Requiring liability insurance only creates an obstacle for people who can't afford to buy it. The result is that only the wealthier people can afford to keep their dogs. Thus, this type of law discriminates against people who are on lower income levels. If I wanted to own a gun and was required to buy an insurance policy to own one and I could not afford this insurance policy, then the only obstacle to owning a gun, my Second Amendment right, is the fact that I can't afford the insurance policy. In other words, state lawmakers are passing laws that include (expensive) insurance requirements only to deny people with lower incomes the same rights as people with higher incomes. This is not about dog ownership.

I filed lawsuits seeking relief from the FDFS's violations of my constitutional rights by deleting me from the licensee database. I was eventually granted relief. But the FDFS then retaliated against me and violated my constitutional rights to fabricate fraudulent court documents. The FDFS then sent these fraudulent court document,s that they knew were fraudulently-obtained, outside of Florida to cause harm to me in other states in which I conduct business.

In 2013, the Indiana insurance commissioner ("IIC") relied upon these fraudulent Florida court documents to seek to punish me even though the Florida situation had nothing to do with Indiana.

However, the IIC twisted the issues to give the false impression that he feared that I would hurt or had hurt an Indiana consumer. There was a fake hearing at the office of the IIC in 2013. I call it a "fake" hearing because the "judge" was an employee of the IIC who cannot be impartial because the IIC pays her salary. But this hearing was conducted by telephone and the hearing was being recorded by both a court reporter in Indiana and by me via telephone. At one point, the court reporter left the "court" in Indiana so that the parties could discuss a "settlement". The counsel for the IIC (Michael Mullen, another employee of the IIC) admitted during this "settlement" discussion that the "commissioner" was not concerned about any alleged injury that I had caused an Indiana resident and that the "commissioner" was mainly concerned about [enforcing] the [fraudulent] court orders arising from Orange County Florida Circuit Court case 2009-CA-037513. This violates the U.S. Constitution for many reasons such as the fact that the IIC has no authority to attempt to enforce a Florida court order. Obviously, the IIC, had abused his authority to fake an administrative action against me in Indiana only to support the fraudulent court orders arising from Florida. Even though the court reporter had left the room in Indiana, I kept recording the telephone call. And I recorded these statements and can present them as evidence. The IIC knows that I have this evidence. The Attorney General of Indiana knows this. As a result, the Indiana state courts have locked me out of the courts completely by literally refusing to docket petitions I have filed seeking relief. As the record in Indiana Supreme Court record 49 S 00 - 1307-OR-00480 shows, I have been locked out of the Indiana state courts.

But the record in the hearing with the IIC establishes that an employee of the IIC, Ronda Ankney, violated many laws when she contacted an insurance company that issued an insurance policy for an Indiana resident and told that insurance company that the Indiana resident had pit bull dogs. Ms. Ankney had no proof of this and she had no right to violate the insured's privacy rights to intervene in this insured's contract. But she did and the insurance company canceled the insurance policy on the basis that the insured had "PITBULL AND THE APPLICANT DOES NOT HAVE A QUALIFYING INSURANCE SCORE". Ms. Ankney obtained proof of this cancellation. She then sent such proof to the local animal control office. The local animal control officer seized the dog owner's dogs only because the dog owner did not have liability insurance for them (which Ms. Ankney caused to be canceled). These dogs had never been aggressive. The insurance was required only due to a local ordinance. The dog owner was unable to obtain another insurance policy fast enough, and the dogs were euthanized by the local animal control office only because the dog owner did not have liability insurance for her dogs. And the dogs were not pit bulls. They were shar peis.

Not long after, I found a letter on my front lawn in Virginia from the IIC, with no postage on it, that demanded that I take down my website www.DangerousDogInsurance.com® . The IIC has no authority to make such a demand. But this letter from the IIC proves that the IIC abused his authority to impede interstate commerce in the insurance industry. And this can easily be classified as a federal crime. And he also abused his authority to injure an Indiana insured only because she owned two Shar pei's.

The issue here is not about dogs. It is about the U.S. Constitution and the fact that many government officials have absolutely abandoned it. It is unconstitutional to make a law that requires a dog owner to obtain liability insurance, and attach penalties for non-compliance without also providing a state-established insurance program from which the dog owner can obtain the insurance. In Massachusetts, for example, the law that requires a dog owner to obtain liability insurance states that the requirement can be met by showing that an attempt was made to procure such insurance (and that no penalties would apply if a dog owner was unable to procure such insurance through no fault of his own).

The various state insurance regulators have learned over time that any administrative interaction with me will almost always reveal evidence that I can use to show the criminal conspiracy arising from Florida to impede interstate commerce and to monopolize the insurance industry for dog owners.

As a result, various state insurance regulators who have chosen to pursue fraudulent actions against me have taken many, many different steps to deny my right to appear at the hearing during which accusations against me are made. (They have also ignored or denied my request for records under the state freedom of information acts.) This denies me the right to cross examine witnesses. I have been able to uncover a great deal of evidence against my accusers through cross examination. But denying me my constitutional right to cross-examine witnesses has enabled the various state insurance commissioners to render me defenseless to their attacks upon me. And the point here is that no matter how much evidence I obtain in my favor, government officials will abuse their authority again and again to deny me even a morsel of relief. This is not the way a democracy works. It is more like the way Communism works.

China's Article 105 of the Criminal Law is as follows: "Criminalizes organizing, scheming or acting to subvert the political power of the state and overthrow the socialist system and incitement to subvert the political power of the state and overthrow the socialist system by spreading rumors, slander or other means."

Despite the fact that China's constitution guarantees the right to free speech and expression, like the U.S. Constitution, this Article 105 of the Criminal Law has been used to allow the state to suppress all criticism of the government. Many Chinese residents who criticized the government have been charged and convicted of "subversion".

Frankly, this is no different from the way I have been treated in the United States of America. While I have not been charged with subversion, various public officials have completely abandoned the U.S. Constitution to arrest me, jail me, freeze my bank accounts, cut the locks off the door of my house to enter to kidnap me, steal real estate from me and more.

And this happens all the time in the United States of America. But not all victims of such abuse write a book about it or make the national news.

The lesson here is that various government officials have and will violate the U.S. Constitution to deny a citizen his most basic rights. And various insurance regulators have, and often do, violate laws to cause injury to citizens in favor of impeding interstate commerce and monopolizing the insurance industry. Most of the time, I offer the least expensive options in the United States of America for dog owners wanting liability insurance. And the insurance regulators don't want dog owners to be able to obtain such liability insurance. In fact, many states have laws that explicitly make it impossible to obtain such liability insurance.

Virginia Code § 3.2–6540 (F) requires some dog owners to procure liability insurance. Virginia Code § 38.2-2128 specifically allows an insurance company to exclude a dog from an insurance policy under certain conditions. The liability insurance requirement under Virginia Code § 3.2–6540 (F) was made law in 1997 and the liability exclusion under Virginia Code § 38.2-2128 was made law in 2004. When Virginia Code § 38.2-2128 was made law in 2004, the "liability insurance" requirement of Virginia Code § 3.2–6540 (F) was rendered unconstitutional.

As another example, Rhode Island has a law that requires certain dog owners to procure liability insurance but has no laws restricting exclusions from the liability insurance policies for these same certain dog owners. And many insurance companies who offer insurance policies to Rhode Island residents exclude from liability coverage certain breeds of dogs, exclude dogs with any prior incidents, and exclude other certain classes of dogs.

Other countries have addressed the "dangerous dog" issue on a national basis. The breeding, importing, and exporting of certain breeds of dogs are banned in many countries. But the U.S. Congress has refused to take up such an important national issue; leaving various states to act surreptitiously in violation of the U.S. Constitution.

And this brings me to the conclusion of this book: the foundation upon which the United States of America was founded. The true impetus to the American Revolution was not the issue of "taxation without representation". The historical recollection referred to as the Gaspee Affair explores the true beginning of the American Revolution. There is a wealth of resources available regarding the Gaspee Affair. But to sum it up: the colonists were restricted by King George III to import items only from England. But the colonists didn't like this restriction and engaged in smuggling of items. The Majesty's navy took action to end this smuggling and stopped all ships en route to the colonies for inspection. Smuggled items were seized. Many residents of Rhode Island, including the governor and other public officials, were tired of the Majesty's navy confiscating the smuggled goods. Residents of Rhode Island planned to attach the Majesty's ship, the Gaspee, one night on June 10, 1772. They attacked it, burned it, and shot its captain. Rhode Island public officials covered up the crimes in many ways: various public officials, including the governor, pretended to be actively investigating the incident. But the truth was that the same public officials were intimidating witnesses. As a result, many years passed and nobody was criminally charged. And nearly every Rhode Island politician celebrates the Gaspee Affair as a wonderful moment in history that sparked the beginning of the U.S.A.

This reveals that many U.S. Historians celebrate 1) greed, 2) a willingness to attack and kill anyone who gets in the way of such desires, and 3) public officials who abuse their authority to commit and cover up crimes. This is the character of the United States of America. And if you are going to challenge questionable or criminal activities of any public official or government body in any way, you can expect retaliation and serious consequences. Hopefully, this book has given you sufficient tools so that you can survive and write your own book to share helpful tips with others who are facing the same obstacles.

Appendix A

2185 RAYBURN HOUSE OFFICE BUILDING
WASHINGTON, DC 20515-0540
(202) 225-4111
FAX (202) 226-0335

1110 E. CHAPMAN AVENUE
SUITE 207
ORANGE, CALIFORNIA 92866
(714) 744-4130
FAX (714) 744-4056

www.royce.house.gov

UNITED STATES
HOUSE OF REPRESENTATIVES

FOREIGN AFFAIRS
Subcommittee
Chairman, Terrorism,
Nonproliferation, and Trade
Asia and the Pacific

FINANCIAL SERVICES
Subcommittee
Capital Markets and
Government Sponsored Enterprises
Financial Institutions and
Consumer Credit

EDWARD R. ROYCE
Fortieth District-California

February 28, 2012

Honorable Kevin M. McCarty, Florida Insurance Commissioner and NAIC President
Dr. Therese M. Vaughan, NAIC CEO
National Association of Insurance Commissioners
444 North Capitol Street NW, Suite 701
Washington, D.C. 20001

Dear Commissioner McCarty and Dr. Vaughan:

As you may know, I am very interested in advancing positive regulatory reform to effect better insurance regulation for consumers. I have supported various efforts to advance reform for many years and look forward to considering the recommendations for improving and modernizing the existing system that the new Federal Insurance Office is scheduled to provide to Congress in the coming days.

In light of the need to reform the existing system, I read with interest a recent press report regarding the National Association of Insurance Commissioners' "initiative to brand itself as a 'standard-setting organization' rather than a trade group."[1] The article states that, at a recent Treasury Department meeting, NAIC members objected to conference participants' description of your Association as a "trade association."

It has been my understanding that the NAIC is a private, 501(c)(3) corporation. Numerous courts, including the U.S. Supreme Court, have quoted from the legislative history of the McCarran Ferguson Act the categorical statement that "[n]othing in the proposed law would ... authorize any private group or association to regulate in the field of interstate commerce."[2] By most accounts, the NAIC is an organization with a $70 million budget not subject to governmental accountability mechanisms such as appropriation oversight and freedom of information act and open meetings laws.

---

[1] Elizabeth Festa and Arthur D. Postal, "Is the NAIC a Trade Group or Official Standard-Setter?", National Underwriter, Dec. 19, 2011.

[2] *FTC v. Travelers*, 362 U.S. 293 (1960). *See also American General v. F.T.C.*, 359 F.Supp. 887 (D.C. Tex. 1973); *U.S. v. Chicago Title*, 242 F.Supp. 56 (D.C. Ill. 1965) (same).

In fact, when challenged regarding its failure to abide by the sorts of accountability statutes that its members must follow in their individual capacities, the NAIC renounced any formal role in the regulatory system. For instance, when the National Conference of Insurance Legislators (NCOIL) challenged the extent of NAIC's authority and influence, and its lack of traditional accountability mechanisms, NAIC replied:

> The NAIC is a 501(c)(3) non-profit corporation. ... As such, the NAIC is not subject to state Open Meetings or 'Sunshine' Laws. ... When individual insurance commissioners gather as members of the NAIC, they are not considered a governmental or public body ... but rather are a private group. As an organization, the NAIC does not have any regulatory authority.[3]

It appears, when it suits its purposes, the NAIC fends off questions about its accountability and transparency by arguing that it is "a private group" that "does not have any regulatory authority." This position is legally essential since, under controlling law, no "private group or association [may] regulate in the field of interstate commerce."

But it would now appear this "traditional" position is politically inconvenient given its attempts to posture itself in the new Dodd-Frank/FIO regime. Present circumstances call for an opposite spin, emphasizing NAIC's key role in "form[ing] the national system of state-based insurance regulation in the U.S."

The NAIC's about-face on its self-proclaimed status in a period of just ten days last summer may best illustrate what appears to be an untenable position. On July 28, 2011 before the House Financial Services Committee, NAIC president, Susan Voss, stated that the NAIC was not part of "some kind of ... national regulatory system"[4] in response to a question regarding its perceived status as a regulatory body lacking traditional accountability. Yet, on August 7, 2011, in what appears to be an effort to demonstrate its relevance in the Dodd-Frank/FIO world, the NAIC claimed it was integral to helping "form the national system of state-based insurance regulation in the U.S"[5] in an attempt to sell the importance of its pronouncement regarding the financial system. These positions seem, at the least, inconsistent.

Given the impending FIO report to Congress on the state of the U.S. regulatory system, understanding precisely what the NAIC is and how it is governed—and reconciling the NAIC's own inherently inconsistent statements about itself—is timely and relevant. Therefore, I ask the following questions.

1. What is NAIC's status? Is it a trade association? Is it a formal part of "the national system of state-based insurance regulation in the U.S."? If so, why did it (a) testify to Congress, when asked specifically about its status, that it does not "hold ourselves out as

---

[3] NAIC president Walter Bell letter to NCOIL president Patrick Kennedy, April 9, 2007.

[4] Hearing transcript at 19. http://financialservices.house.gov/UploadedFiles/112-53.pdf

[5] NAIC press release of Aug. 7, 2011.
See http://www.naic.org/Releases/2011_docs/naic_response_credit_downgrade.htm.

some kind of ... national regulatory system"; and (b) insist to NCOIL that it is "not considered a ... public body" and "does not have any regulatory authority"?

2. Does NAIC agree that as a self-described "private group," it may not "regulate in the field of interstate commerce"? Do its activities—including but not limited to the Securities Valuation Office, System for Electronic Rate and Form Filing, Financial Standards and Accreditation Program, Market Analysis Procedures Working Group, and National Insurance Producer Registry—amount to regulating interstate commerce and/or exercising governmental authority under color of law?

3. As a 501(c)(3) non-profit corporation, does the NAIC not file a Form 990, a routine financial statement for non-profits, with the Internal Revenue Service (IRS)? If the NAIC has been formally exempted by the IRS from filling this information, please provide written documentation of this exemption, and explain why the NAIC feels it necessary to keep this disclosure from public scrutiny.

I would appreciate your prompt attention to this matter and a substantive written reply.

Sincerely,

EDWARD R. ROYCE

NAIC National Association of Insurance Commissioners

& The CENTER for INSURANCE POLICY and RESEARCH

March 20, 2012

The Honorable Edward R. Royce
U.S. House of Representatives
2185 Rayburn House Office Building
Washington, DC 20515-0540

Dear Mr. Royce,

I am in receipt of your letter dated February 28 and I am happy to respond to your inquiries concerning the National Association of Insurance Commissioners (NAIC). The NAIC was organized in 1871 by the chief insurance regulators of the states to exchange ideas and information and to promote the uniformity of insurance regulation in policy, laws and regulations where such uniformity is appropriate. In 1999 the NAIC incorporated under the laws of the State of Delaware and was awarded 501(c)(3) tax exempt status shortly thereafter. Membership in the NAIC is voluntary; however, all 50 states, the District of Columbia and five US territories are represented. More than 4000 state statutes, regulations, bulletins, attorney general opinions and court cases reference the NAIC. The NAIC supports the insurance regulatory work of its members providing services and systems that would otherwise fall to the states to develop individually.

At the outset, it appears there may be some confusion regarding the role of the NAIC in the national state based system of insurance regulation and I hope this letter serves as sufficient clarification for you. The NAIC as an association does not have regulatory authority, but its members do. The association does provide a forum for members to establish regulatory policy, standards, and best practices. However, the decision to implement such standards remains with the individual states. The NAIC therefore does play an integral role in the national system of state based regulation as a forum for standard setting, but it is not a regulator. There can be confusion when collective state regulatory actions developed at an NAIC meeting are mistakenly referred to as actions "of the NAIC" in the press or elsewhere, but at no time has the organization itself represented that it is a regulator. This is consistent both with Commissioner Voss's testimony, which indicated the NAIC as an association is not a national or federal regulator, and the NAIC press release you cited in your letter which mentioned the role centralized resources of the NAIC play in assisting state regulators in carrying out their regulatory function.

I will now turn to responding to some of the specific issues you have raised:

The NAIC's legal status is a Delaware non-profit corporation recognized as a 501(c)(3) by the Internal Revenue Service. The NAIC is not a trade association and you are correct that members of the NAIC object to its characterization as such. A trade association is made up of businesses or business people in a common field and is designed to assist its members and its industry in dealing with mutual business problems. The NAIC is an association of elected and appointed state regulatory officials charged with regulating the insurance industry under state law.

EXECUTIVE OFFICE · 444 North Capitol Street, NW, Suite 701 · Washington, DC 20001-1509   p | 202 471 3990   f | 816 460 7493
CENTRAL OFFICE · 1100 Walnut Street, Suite 1500 · Kansas City, MO 64106-2197   p | 816 842 3600   f | 816 783 8175
CAPITAL MARKETS & INVESTMENT ANALYSIS OFFICE · 48 Wall Street, 6th Floor · New York, NY 10005-2906   p | 212 398 9000   f | 212 382 4207

www.naic.org

Specifically, the NAIC is organized for the purposes of:

> ". . . assisting state insurance regulators, individually and collectively, in serving the public interest and achieving the following fundamental insurance regulatory goals: a) protect the public interest, promote competitive markets and facilitate the fair and equitable treatment of insurance consumers; b) promote, in the public interest, the reliability, solvency and financial solidity of insurance institutions; and c) support and improve state regulation of insurance." (Source: NAIC Articles of Incorporation)

You mention the oral testimony of Commissioner Voss in response to a question from Congressman Dold. Commissioner Voss's full response, according to the transcript was as follows:

> "The NAIC is really our organization that helps us put standards together, standard setting, and sort of collectively represents what our thoughts are. We don't put ourselves out as some regulatory body. Having said that, I think through even Federal regulation laws, if you look at the Health Care Reform Act, the NAIC has been asked to set standards for certain processes under PPACA. And so collectively, the regulators get together and discuss those. But we don't hold ourselves out as some kind of Federal or national regulatory system. We are a national body that represents all of the regulators."

Commissioner Voss clearly makes the point that the NAIC is not a regulatory body, though she mistakenly uses the word "system" at the end of her response where the word "body" would be more appropriate. We appreciate the opportunity to clarify that word choice and apologize for any confusion it may have caused you.

The NAIC as a non-profit corporation does not have regulatory authority, and I am not aware that it has ever presented itself as having such authority. However, its membership is composed of individuals that do have such authority and the NAIC provides a forum and vehicle for its membership to develop standards and collectively set regulatory policy including serving as its members' collective voice, crafting models laws and guidelines, coordinating examinations, and consulting each other regarding regulatory actions.

The NAIC activities you have identified do not amount to regulating interstate commerce or exercising regulatory authority as the NAIC simply provides these resources to assist the states in carrying out their regulatory functions.

You have identified several NAIC programs which are explained as follows:

- The Securities Valuation Office (SVO) is a division within the NAIC that conducts credit quality assessment and valuation of securities owned by state regulated insurance companies. Insurance companies report ownership of securities to the SVO as part of their annual financial statement filings which are mandated by the states. The SVO conducts credit analysis on these securities for the purpose of assigning an NAIC designation and/or unit price. These designations and unit prices are produced solely for the benefit of state insurance departments who may utilize them as part of the state's monitoring of the financial condition of its domiciliary insurers.

- System for Electronic Rate and Form Filing (SERFF). The NAIC developed this system in 1996 to provide a cost-effective method for handling insurance policy rate and form filings between regulators and insurance companies. The SERFF system is designed to enable companies to send and for states to receive, comment on, and approve or reject insurance industry rate and form filings for their insurance products.

- Financial Standards and Accreditation Program. The NAIC accreditation program establishes and maintains standards to promote sound insurance company financial solvency regulations. These standards are developed by the state regulators who are members of the Financial Standards and Accreditation Committee and then must be approved by a super majority of the entire membership. Through this program, the solvency regulation of multi-state insurance companies is enhanced, made uniform and monitored so that state regulators can rely upon each other to make certain companies licensed and selling insurance in the several states are held to adequate solvency standards through a process of financial analysis and examination performed by the domiciliary state regulators.

- Market Analysis Procedures Working Group. The NAIC's Market Analysis Procedures Working Group (MAP) is the national forum for states to share and coordinate their insurance market analysis programs. The working group, which is made up of state insurance regulators, reviews and coordinates state market analysis programs and develops procedures for uniform, nationwide analysis using their adopted Framework for Market Analysis.

- The National Insurance Producer Registry (NIPR) is a non-profit affiliate of the NAIC incorporated in 1996. NIPR supports the work of the states and the NAIC by providing an electronic means for the submission of insurance producers' licensing and appointment transactions to the states. NIPR is governed by a 13 member board of directors, with six members representing the NAIC, six industry trade association representatives, including three producer trades and the CEO of the NAIC as an ex-officio voting board member.

The NAIC is not required to file a Form 990 pursuant to an Internal Revenue Service (IRS) ruling. The documentation from the IRS exempting the NAIC from that requirement will be provided to your office in hard copy. The NAIC was afforded this exemption in 1955 and it was reaffirmed upon our 1999 incorporation and receipt of tax exempt status.

We share your interest in advancing positive regulatory reform to effect better insurance regulation for consumers. There are a number of initiatives underway individually in the states and through the NAIC that are being developed in exactly this spirit of positive regulatory reform. We welcome the opportunity to discuss our work with you or your staff, though we continue to believe that efforts to refine insurance regulation are and should remain the purview of the states.

I trust this response provides substantive answers to your questions and clarification of statements made in your recent letter to the NAIC. If I can be of further assistance, please contact me.

Sincerely,

Kevin M. McCarty
NAIC President
Florida Insurance Commissioner

Appendix B

The full article can be viewed at this link:

http://www.phyllis-chesler.com/1048/jewish-american-mother-tortured

Last viewed: July 29, 2015.

Jewish-American Mother Tortured in

Solitary Confinement in America Because

She Loves her Daughter

by Phyllis Chesler

November 16, 2011

This is just a summary of the full article:

Valerie Carlton was a resident of Harford County, Maryland. Her then-husband, Russell Carlton, and the judicial and penal authorities in Harford County, Maryland, egregiously violated Ms. Carlton's constitutional rights and human rights only because she "dared to disagree with her husband about the existence of original sin; she believed that people are born innocent, not guilty". Valerie's mother is a Jew. Her father is a Christian. Valerie married Russell Carlton, a Christian. But when Valerie later "began her return to Judaism and began to light Sabbath candles with her daughter present", Russell, and many others, including local lawyers, judges, and law enforcement began a campaign to destroy Ms. Carlton for the purpose of terminating her physical contact with her daughter. Mr. Carlton wanted sole physical custody of their daughter. This campaign included falsely accusing Ms Carlton of sexually abusing her daughter. Ms. Carlton was charged with multiple felony counts all of which were dropped much later after Ms. Carlton had been incarcerated without bail for more than one year. Ms. Carlton was severely abused while incarcerated. Her story shows that the judges, lawyers, and law enforcement agencies (public officials) will not hesitate to abuse their authority to destroy a person's life for the benefit of someone else.

More information can be found at www.ValerieCarlton.com

Appendix C

Taken from:

http://thefullcourtpress.org/the-herb-lux-story-must-see/#

Last viewed July 28, 2015

HERB LUX v. WILLIAM F. NEELY

July 11, 2014   Rhondimon

Since 1992, Herb Lux has been fighting the local Courthouse in Spotsylvania County and specifically, William Neely.   Lux, now 62, has been entangled with Mr Neely in a dance of   criminal charges, appeals, acquittals and as of recently his latest Virginia   Supreme Court Appeal was denied.

In researching the allegations Lux has made against Spotsylvania County and the Commonwealth Attorney, it appears that he is on to something. From a glance at the files and a thorough reading of the transcripts, it doesn't take longer than 5-7 pages into a tight reading, that Neely has it out for Lux and is pushing his weight around in his Official Capacity.

The Charges are obscure, petty and appear frivolous however, not according to the Spotsylvania County magistrates.   Bonds in upwards of $30,000.00 have been assigned to Mr. Lux for offenses such as "Not getting up from the Litigation Table fast enough" and "Having a Police Conversation with a Juror after the Trial was over".

Clearly, these charges are trumped up and wrought with malice against this little elderly man. Almost everytime Lux has been charged – he was convicted in the Circuit Courts. The only place Lux has experienced relief is in the Court of Appeals and the Supreme Court until last week, where the Virginia Supreme Court denied his petition on a Misdemeanor charge lodged by Mr. Neely last year.

TFCP has learned that Neely – unlawfully went behind the defense counsel's back to obtain an Ex Parte hearing with Circuit Court Judge Beck and talked him into "revoking" Lux's appeal bond regardless that Lux has yet to exhaust all Due Process remedies alotted to him.

One would presume that Neely had better use of his time than to exhaust his efforts, devising schemes and engineering plots to destroy Herb Lux. I have met Herb and come to grow quit fond of him. He is a meek, friendly and extremely helpful gentleman. One could only draw the conclusion that Neely is the quintessential Bully and Lux has no choice but to stand-up to him or the abuse and oppression will grow insurmountably worse.

BONUS!!!

Get more than 1000 pages of court documents that have been used and filed in real state and federal court cases, sample forms, and sample petitions for only $9.99 if purchased online at www.PreparingForYourLawsuit.com. You receive electronic copies and you print the documents and forms. Or you pay only $49.99 if purchased in hard-copy form. You receive printed documents and forms in the mail. If you only want documents from a specific case file, the documents can be provided at a cost of $9.99 if by delivered by email. The cost varies if you want the documents mailed.